GW01270981

Modern Poetry in 1

Series Three, Numl

After-Images

Edited by David and Helen Constantine

MODERN POETRY IN TRANSLATION

Modern Poetry in Translation
Series Three, No. 6
© Modern Poetry in Translation 2006 and contributors
ISBN 0-9545367-6-2
ISBN 978-0-9545367-6-3
ISSN 0969-3572

Printed and bound in Great Britain by Short Run Press, Exeter

Editors: David and Helen Constantine
Reviews Editor: Josephine Balmer
Administrators: Deborah de Kock and Angela Holton

Submissions should be sent in hard copy, with return postage, to David
and Helen Constantine, *Modern Poetry in Translation*, The Queen's College,
Oxford, OX1 4AW. Unless agreed in advance, submissions by email will
not be accepted. Only very exceptionally will we consider work that has
already been published elsewhere. Translators are themselves responsible
for obtaining any necessary permissions. Since we do sometimes authorize
further publication on one or two very reputable websites of work that has
appeared in *MPT*, the permissions should cover that possibility.

Founding Editors: Ted Hughes and Daniel Weissbort

Subscription Rates: (including postage)

	UK	Overseas
Single Issue	£11	£13 / US$ 24
One year subscription (2 issues, surface mail)	£22	£26 / US$ 48
Two year subscription (4 issues, surface mail)	£40	£48 / US$ 88

To subscribe please use the subscription form at the back of the magazine.
Discounts available.

To pay by credit card please visit www.mptmagazine.com

Modern Poetry in Translation is represented in UK by Central Books,
99 Wallis Road, London, E9 5LN

For orders: tel +44 (0) 845 458 9910 Fax +44 (0) 845 458 9912
or visit www.mptmagazine.com

Contents

Editorial

Literally, an after-image is 'the impression retained by the retina of the eye, or by any other organ of sense, of a vivid sensation, after the external cause has been removed'. Figuratively, the word is very rich indeed. In the autumn of 1818, Keats, nursing his dying brother Tom and on the threshold of falling in love with Fanny Brawne, borrowed the sonnets of Ronsard, read them closely, and, without the text in front of him, translated one of them. The identity of the foreign sonnet had impressed itself upon him, he worked from the lingering after-image, developing it his own way, and concluding (at the twelfth line, no more were needed) with the astonishing 'Love poured her beauty into my warm veins'. There is no 'warm' in Ronsard's poem, Keats's addition obliges us to feel the incoming of love and beauty as a cold shock. The after-image made flesh again! The following spring, Tom dead, Keats, in thrall to Miss Brawne, was reading Cary's Dante, especially the *Inferno*, Canto V, the Paolo and Francesca episode. When he slept he dreamed himself into that circle, when he woke he wrote a sonnet out of the dream, out of the translation, conjuring the after-images. Five days later he wrote 'La Belle Dame Sans Merci', so full of love and the desolate cold. Keats, self-annihilatingly open to impressions, to identities of people and poems pressing in upon him, suffering afterwards among their after-images, answered back with poems, which is to say with deeds of life, that were all his own. We had a very abundant response to our call for after-images: poems after photos and pictures; ghostings and reincarnations of other writers; conversions of ancient and foreign forms (conversions of their lingering effects into the here and now); memories one would be loath to lose, memories one might wish to erase. After-images, like exile, wandering, the loss and recovery of speech, will be a continuing ingredient in future issues of *MPT*. And rightly. First, because it is a good metaphor of the idea and the practice of translation (whether you have the foreign text in front of you while you work or not). Secondly, because in its literal and in its figurative senses the term touches closely on the writing and the reading of poetry itself. A poem is the conversion into an apt and lasting form of perhaps many impressions, many after-images; is itself then an after-image – that works lingeringly on the consciousness and indeed on the active life of its unimagined readers.

The word holds a utopian possibility too. The image lingers after its physical cause has ceased. Like looking at a bright star, actually dead and lightless. Good people, good ideas, good societies linger on as images long after the bad have defeated and eradicated them. Writers are (among other things) the custodians of potent after-images, and can help them back into life, in effective shapes, here and now.

David and Helen Constantine
September 2006

The next issue of *MPT*

The spring issue of *Modern Poetry in Translation* (Third Series, Number 7) will be called *Love and War*.

We are looking for translations and original poems on this topic – whose two elements might be treated separately or together, as literally or figuratively, as privately or politically, as you please. Ancient and modern variations are equally welcome.

Submissions should be sent by 1 March 2007, in hard copy, with return postage, to The Editors, Modern Poetry in Translation, The Queen's College, Oxford, OX1 4AW. Unless agreed in advance, submissions by email will not be accepted. Only very exceptionally will we consider work that has already been published elsewhere. Translators are themselves responsible for obtaining any necessary permissions. Since we do sometimes authorize further publication on one or two very reputable websites of work that has appeared in *MPT*, the permissions should cover that possibility.

Karen Leeder
Poems after Brecht

14th August 2006 marks the fiftieth anniversary of the death
of the German writer Bertolt Brecht. He is without a doubt the
most important and influential dramatist of the twentieth
century worldwide. His influence extends far beyond Germany
and includes the English-speaking world and much of the
developing world – where his revolutionary politics and
theatrical practice still have a very real and raw energy. But his
legacy as a poet is equally, if not more, important and since
1990 is being rediscovered in a new political climate.

It is not just that Brecht's poems are still read, nor that they
are influential – though they are certainly both of these – but
rather that his poetry has found a further afterlife in the work
of the poets who have come after him. Any list of poets
inspired by Brecht's legacy in Germany is a virtual 'Who's
Who' of German poetry over the last half a century: Wolf

Biermann, Volker Braun, Paul Celan, Hans Magnus
Enzensberger, Günter Kunert, Friederike Mayröcker, or Inge
Müller. But that legacy has also gone on to inspire some of the
most significant younger poets writing today. And, after the
fall of the Berlin Wall, Brecht has been taken up, not only by
the writers who were sympathetic to his Communist ideals, or
lived through the socialist reality they inspired, as one might
expect, but also by younger poets who never knew him and
who do not share his political convictions. That Brecht should
have acted as a focus for so many poems suggests something
more than a simple reading of his work. It has to do with him
as a figure too. His personal charisma, his radical politics, his
wayward behaviour, his desire to rip up any rule books and
change art and the world, have all contributed to a kind of
mythical aura which has engendered reworkings of his life in
novels, films and plays. But also the contradictions, both real
and of biographical anecdote, have become part of a legend: the
young man who could publish a pornographic sonnet under
the name of the venerable (and despised) antagonist Thomas
Mann, the silk shirts under the worker's jacket, the comrade-
ship and faithlessness in the same breath, the unapologetic
public Stalinism and private subversion.

In the Anglophone world his reception has been slower
and more hesitant. The figure of Brecht exerts a powerful
magnetism here as in Germany; and, whether 'loving Brecht'
(the title of Elaine Feinstein's 1992 novel), or hating him – as
in the aggressive and damagingly inaccurate 'Brecht-buster',
John Fuegi's *Life and Lies of Bertolt Brecht* of the same year –
the contradictions and personal charisma of the figure still
fascinate. However, the work (as opposed to the figure) has
been more partially received in English. When the volume of
translations, *Bertolt Brecht: Poems 1913–1956*, edited by John
Willett and Ralph Manheim with the co-operation of Erich
Fried, was published in 1976, it was greeted by extraordinary
reviews: definitive statements from powerful backers: 'A mind-
changing volume, after which, for all but the most parochial

critics, the pecking order in the modern pantheon will never be the same' (Kenneth Tynan); 'It is clear that Brecht was that very rare phenomenon: a great poet for whom poetry is an almost everyday visitation and drawing of breath' (George Steiner). However, it would be fair to say that his poetry is far less well known in this country. There are many reasons for this; some of them practical, to do with the timing of translations, and the power of the Brecht estate. But there is also something more fundamental. It is clear that he has a reputation as an austere poet, intellectual, emotionally cold, and fiercely political, with no time for the affect or subjectivity often associated with the roots of the lyric genre. But it also has to do with his unique diction. Brecht was a superb lyric poet who profoundly distrusted the lyric mode. Nature and love are at the centre of his work and yet he wrote with a conviction that it was largely illegitimate in times like his to derive poetry from such experiences. That he managed to articulate this contradiction has much to do with his 'cunning' – Brecht's word is 'List' – a project which also became a philosophy of survival for him in the Third Reich. He borrowed and adapted traditional forms but also created new lyric structures and an immediately recognisable voice: low-key, simple, but without being arch or sentimental.

If that aesthetic took him outside the mainstream of English language poetry, nevertheless one finds the debt to his work in sometimes unexpected places. One of the most striking passages in Bob Dylan's *Chronicles* (2004), for example, concerns a production of *The Threepenny Opera* and the almost physical blow the singer felt on first hearing a performance of the 'Song of Pirate Jenny': 'Within a few minutes I felt like I hadn't slept or tasted food for about thirty hours.' Later, having worked on the song, 'unzipped it' as he says, he found the structures revealed: 'Everything was fastened to the wall with a heavy bracket, but you couldn't see what the sum total of all the parts were, not unless you stood way back and waited 'til the end. It was like the Picasso painting Guernica.' One might naturally make a casual link between Brecht and Dylan, charismatic passionate singer-poets of the Left, but it is unlikely one would have seen the origins of songs like 'Lonesome Death of Hattie Carroll', 'Who Killed Davey Moore', 'Only a Pawn in Their Game' or 'A Hard Rain's A-Gonna Fall' in Brecht as Dylan himself does. 'If I hadn't gone to the Theatre de Lys and heard the ballad 'Pirate Jenny', it might not have dawned on me to write them, that songs like these could be written.'

There are perhaps two further reasons why Brecht has provoked such a particular and vigorous response. He is also a poet's poet – in the best sense of the phrase. Although he was a writer urgently concerned with the dark times he lived in, very many of his poems are also themselves about poetry, or P^2, as Erich Fried, one of Brecht's most diligent readers, called it. And it is for that reason too that those who have come after have felt themselves called on to respond both to their own times and to the demands of poetry. But finally: the real test of any poet's longevity is the extent to which the work touches some real core of recognition. Ironically Brecht hoped, in one famous poem, that posterity would simply not recognise the world he described, because they would live in a truly humane society of the future. But if the end of the Cold War has superficially appeared to legitimize prejudices against Brecht's Marxist politics, in fact one is constantly made aware of the continuing relevance of Brecht's concerns. He wanted to make people ask questions of the world and themselves. In a world of increasing economisation, globalisation and self-governing and inscrutable power structures, Brecht demands that we look beyond the surface of power to discover the real interests at work.

It is commonly argued that Brecht's drama (on the surface more openly and specifically political) has been compromised by the failure of the system it advocated; while his poetry, with its clean, lyrical lines has survived unscathed. But that is an oversimplification on many levels. A version of Brechtian

drama flourishes everywhere in the West, from the subsidised
stage to the temples of the West End. Equally, his questions
about justice, warfare, capitalism and power can be asked anew
of our own dark times. But, in any case, the poetry and the
plays are not that distinct. Both, but perhaps especially his
poetry, touch on love, beauty and humanity. But for Brecht
these are intrinsically political things in that they provide a
militant answer to the dark times around him. His famous line
from 1930, 'Change the world: it needs it' still rings true, even
if some of the players in that world have changed.

That relevance is demonstrated by the poems presented here
by poets commissioned to take part in the Poetry International
event in October in the Purcell Room. Poetry International,
the South Bank Centre's biennial festival celebrating poetry
from around the world, now traditionally dedicates an evening
to feature new poems written by leading contemporary poets in
honour of a great poet whose legacy still inspires us today. For
previous festivals there have been evenings dedicated to Dante,
Lorca, and Akhmatova. This year, to mark the fiftieth
anniversary of his death, the poet who has been chosen is
Bertolt Brecht. This choice is a perhaps a conscious nod to the
origins of the festival at the height of the Cold War, when Ted
Hughes and Patrick Garland were concerned to bring dissident
voices to a western audience. But what better moment too, to
re-examine the stature of this most iconic figure?

My interest in the project came from my experience of
editing an anthology of international poems with a German
colleague, Erdmut Wizisla, the head of the Brecht archive in
Berlin: *O Chicago! O Widerspruch!: Ein Hundert Gedichte auf
Brecht* (*O Chicago O Dialectic: One hundred poems for Brecht*) and
an anthology of translations for Carcanet: *After Brecht: A
Celebration*. This is in some ways an extension of those under-
takings, in that it has involved commissioning new poems by
leading poets from the UK and Germany: Ulrike Draesner,
Albert Ostermaier, Bert Papenfuss, David Constantine, Andy
Croft, Lavinia Greenlaw and Adrian Mitchell. The German

poets, though individually very different, had all engaged with Brecht to some degree in the past: indeed Albert Ostermaier curated a five-day festival of Brecht's poetry in Augsburg this July. The English poets too had different experiences with Brecht: from David Constantine, who, as an academic had written on the poet over many years, to Lavinia Greenlaw, who was inspired by the diction of individual poems. The German poets worked with distinguished translators and poets Iain Galbraith, Tom Cheesman and Andrew Duncan. All of the English poets had access to the monumental edition of *Poems*, edited by John Willett; and I provided literal versions where necessary. Everyone was given a free hand; and the responses vary accordingly in their tone and their proximity to Brecht: from translations of individual poems to versions which take up Brecht's originals in a much looser way, responses to Brecht as a figure, or to quotations from his work and poems written in an idiom which might be defined as Brechtian. They range too in the 'Brecht' that has caught their eye: from exuberant early balladeer to the classical austerity of the later poet. It is striking that poems which face the explicitly political Brecht head-on and reinterpret his gesture for our own bleak times, stand next to experimental reflections and much quieter meditations on traditional themes.

Adrian Mitchell offers a new translation of Brecht's 'Von der Kindesmörderin Marie Farrar' ('Of the Infanticide Marie Farrar'), a poem which has inspired his own writing in the past, and also shares a concern with 'humanity', or rather the failure of it, in his own poem 'The baby on the pavement'. This lucid report on 'Human Nature' perhaps draws too on Brecht's play *The Caucasian Chalk Circle*, where goodness brings its own particular punishments: 'Terrible is the temptation to good!' Andy Croft also turns to the early Brecht: providing a sharply humorous response to the famous 'The Ballad of Mack the Knife' from the *Threepenny Opera*. Brecht's poem, a ruthless send-up of Weimar cabaret songs, has ironically become one of the most-recorded standards in the history of pop music, but is returned there to its darkly sardonic origins. Lavinia Greenlaw's 'On Spring' turns to Brecht's 'Concerning Spring', a typically brutal 1920s poem welcoming the annual burst of 'irresistible violent leafing of trees' that the concrete jungles conceal from us, but offers something more elusive and alienated, as does her 'Love Poem' which draws inspiration from Brecht's 'Liebesgedicht' of 1925. In Albert Ostermaier's 'offside trap or: brecht finds benn' Brecht commends to Gottfried Benn the healing gravity of football. In the World Cup year, this casts an ironic perspective on the rivalry between Brecht and the West German poet Benn, who became very important after the Second World War. He represented in almost every respect the complete opposite of Brecht in his dark, highly rhetorical, 'monologic' poetry. In the GDR Brecht would dedicate a pointed verse to him, 'Listening to verses by the death-obsessed Gottfried Benn', in which he noted on the faces of the workers an 'expression that was more priceless than the Mona Lisa'. But Ostermaier also takes up Brecht's 'Hollywood Elegies', famously set to music by Hanns Eisler, when Brecht, struggling in exile to become a script writer, saw Hollywood as a kind of hell and everyone there as prostitutes selling their souls. Ulrike Draesner, writing from Svendborg, where Brecht's refuge in exile is now a writer's centre, offers a sequence of poems on Brecht's relationship with the Danish novelist, actress, photographer, and director, Ruth Berlau, who became known as 'Red Ruth' because of her antifascist commitment and work with the Danish resistance during the war. Her life was irrevocably marked by her meeting with Brecht in 1933, and she travelled with him from Denmark to the United States and to the GDR collaborating with him, inspired him and loving him, before a final break and a miserable and lonely death in Berlin in 1974. David Constantine's 'Quatrains for a Primer of our Times' draw on Brecht's own *Kriegsfibel* (*War Primer*), a collection of what Brecht called 'photo-epigrams' – four-line verses captioning photographs clipped from newspapers and magazines. They were mainly composed during World War II, while Brecht was living in Scandinavia and the United States as an exile and were edited by Berlau, before finally being published as a book in 1955 in the GDR. In her introductory note, Berlau challenges the idea that the meaning of a press photograph is self-evident: Brecht's book is offered, therefore, as a practical manual, demonstrating how to 'read' or 'translate' press photographs. At the same time, it seeks to provide some basic lessons about the nature of modern warfare; lessons, it seems, that still need to be learned, as these new poems demonstrate. Constantine's other poem offers a Brechtian view of a post-1990 Germany, something that has also inspired the poet Bert Papenfuss. Once one of the most innovative voices of the underground poetry scene of East Berlin, Papenfuss has established himself as the most clear-sighted and sharp-tongued critic of the united Germany. His letter to Brecht addresses the poet with his given name 'Eugen Berthold', a name swiftly abandoned when Brecht reinvented himself as a cool, metropolitan poet. But if Papenfuss quotes Brecht's famous poem 'Vom armen B.B.' ('Of poor B.B.'), it is with little sympathy and even less for the corruptions of the present. That Brecht's poetry can still nevertheless inspire resistance to that reality is signalled by the title of his second poem: 'With all your might', perhaps the most fiercely revolutionary of all the poems here.

But these poems are only a sample of the work that has been going on this year, and a foretaste of the reading which will take place in October: proof, if it were needed, of Brecht's lasting legacy and relevance. 'In the dark times / Will there also be singing?' asked Brecht in 1938. 'Yes, there will also be singing/ About the dark times.' It seems Brecht was right.

The reading 'To Those Born Later' will take place at 7.45 pm on Friday October 27th in the Purcell Room, The South Bank, with David Constantine, Andy Croft, Ulrike Draesner, Lavinia Greenlaw, Adrian Mitchell, Albert Ostermaier, and Bert Papenfuss. It will be preceded by a discussion with the poets, 'Brecht's Poetic Legacy', chaired by Karen Leeder.

Adrian Mitchell
Two Poems

About the child-murderer Marie Farrar

1.

Marie Farrar, aged sixteen.
No criminal record up to now,
Orphan, with rickets; birthmarks, none –
Killed a baby – this is how:
In her second month, as she reports it,
A woman in a basement room
Gave two injections to abort it.
Which hurt, she says, but the child stayed in her womb.
   But you, please don't be angry or upset.
   We all need all the help that we can get.

2.

Anyway, she says, she paid,
Then laced her corset very tight,
Drank schnapps with pepper, but that only made
Her vomit half the night.
Now her belly was visibly swollen.
Doing the washing up was agony.
She was, she says, a young girl and still growing.
She prayed to Mary, optimistically.
    You too, please don't be angry or upset.
    We all need all the help that we can get.

3.

Her prayers, apparently, were useless.
Maybe she'd asked too much. She put on weight.
At early mass her head was full of dizziness,
She knelt at the altar covered in cold sweat.
But still she kept her condition secret
Till, later on, birth took her by surprise.
She was so plain that nobody imagined
Sexual temptation could arise.
    And you, please don't be angry or upset.
    We all need all the help that we can get.

4.

On the day itself, she says, just about dawn
She was scrubbing the stairs, when suddenly
Great talons clawed at her guts. She was all torn.
But still, she kept the secret of her pregnancy.
All the time she was hanging out the washing,
She thought it out – she had to be delivered
And very soon. Her heart was heavy.
She finished work late, then went up to bed.
    But you, please don't be angry or upset.
    We all need all the help that we can get.

5.

As she lay down, they called her. Right away!
Sweep up the newly-fallen snow!
That took until eleven. It was a long day,
No time to give birth till past midnight. And so
She brought forth, so she says, a son.
This son was like all others that are born.
But she was unlike other mothers – though
I find I cannot think of her with scorn.
 You too, please don't be angry or upset.
 We all need all the help that we can get.

6.

So now I'd like to go on telling
The story of what happened to this son,
(She wants, she says, not to hide anything),
So what I am and what you are is clear to everyone.
She'd just climbed into bed, when she felt sick.
She was all alone. She wanted to shout.
She didn't know what was going to happen
But managed to stop herself crying out.
 And you, please don't be angry or upset.
 We all need all the help that we can get.

7.

Her room was cold as ice, so she,
With her last strength, crawled to the lavatory
And there, she doesn't know when exactly,
Gave birth to a son without ceremony
Just before morning. She was, she says,
All muddled up. She didn't know
If her freezing hands could hold on to the child
Because the servants' toilet was adrift with snow.
 You too, please don't feel angry or upset.
 We all need all the help that we can get.

8.

Between her own room and the outdoor privy.
(Nothing happened till this point, she insists),
The child started crying unbearably, so she
Beat it, blindly, without stopping, with both fists,
And went on beating it till it was quiet, she says.
And then she took it into bed
And kept it with her all through the night
And hid it, the next morning, in a shed.
But you, please don't be angry or upset.
We all need all the help that we can get.

9.

Marie Farrar, aged sixteen,
Died in the Meissen jail.
What does this guilty mother's story mean?
It shows all creatures of the earth are frail.
You who give birth in clean and comfortable beds
And call your pregnancy a blessed state,
Do not condemn the wretched and the weak –
Their sins are heavy, but their suffering is great.
And so, please don't be angry or upset.
We all need all the help that we can get.

(A translation of Brecht's 'Von der Kindesmörderin Marie
Farrar')

The Baby on the Pavement

People keep telling me about Human Nature
and how vile it is.
I have made up this story for them:

There is a naked baby
lying on the pavement.

No, the naked baby
is lying on a blanket
on the pavement.
(I find I can't leave it there
without a blanket,
even in a story.)

Watch the first human being
who comes walking down the pavement.

Does he step over the baby and walk on?
Does he kick the baby and walk on?

He picks up the baby,
wraps it in the blanket
and tries to find somebody
to help him look after the baby.

Isn't that your Human Nature?

Andy Croft
Two Poems

An Offer You Can't Refuse

*'If sharks ruled the world they would teach the little fish that
it is a great honour to swim into the mouth of a shark.'* (Brecht)

As the actress takes the curtain
They are cheering in the stalls,   ·
Mack the Knife is out of town, dear,
Though his name's sprayed on the walls.

O the shark has pretty teeth, dear,
And he shows them pearly white,
But on the east side of this town, dear,
You can walk home safe at night.

Here the shark is just a story,
Some old song about some teeth,
But there's some who think that freedom's
Just a name for old Macheath.

On the radio, Sunday morning,
Frank Sinatra swings this town;
You had better watch your back, dear,
When the walls start tumbling down.

Now the banks are full of money
And the streets are full of life;
But who's that sneaking round the corner –
Is that someone Mack the Knife?

All the ladies love a blade, dear,
And the whole world loves a knave,
But he'll leave you lying bleeding
And he'll put you in your grave.

You are free to spend your savings
On expensive merchandise,
And you're free to walk the streets, dear,
Because freedom has its price.

When the shark bites with his teeth, dear,
Scarlet billows start to spread,
On the streets young men are shouting,
A foreign student turns up dead.

Now the knives are coming out, dear,
And the sharp suits cut like glass,
And there's beggars in the subways
On the razor edge of class.

Unemployment keeps on rising,
While the dole keeps going down –
Oh, the line forms on the right, dear,
Now that Mackie – yes good old Mackie
Now that Mackie is back in town.

Forces
(After Bert Ward)

There you stood, armed with only a few poems
Against all the forces of money.

There you stood, armed with only a few poems
Against all the forces of injustice and money.

There you stood, armed with only a few poems
Against all the forces of reaction, injustice and money.

There you stood, armed with only a few poems
Against all the forces of hunger, reaction, injustice
    and money.

There you stood, armed with only a few poems
Against all the forces of oppression, hunger, reaction,
    injustice and money.

There you stood, armed with only a few poems
Against all the forces of fascism, oppression, hunger,
    reaction, injustice and money.

There you stood, armed with only a few poems
Against all the forces of war, fascism, oppression, hunger,
    reaction, injustice and money.
And there your enemies stood,
Armed with all the forces
Of money, injustice, reaction, hunger,
Oppression, fascism and war,
Against only a few poems.

Lavinia Greenlaw
Brecht Variations

Love Poem

No call, yet he waits in this unmade house
for something which, he can feel it, has taken a step
and is making its way towards this unmade house
towards its first night in the open.

He checks around, the place is still empty.
It will be as unlived-in tomorrow as today
no more than room for him to inhabit, him alone.
To make sure of this, he takes down the moon.

Yet what if it has no sense of direction?
He is learning but tonight gets the lesson wrong
and persuades himself that he must sleep or else
it may take fright and turn from the door.

On Spring

Way back when we first seized upon
oil, iron and ammonia, each year
brought about the incxorable, forceful
greening of trees. We can all remember
enlarged days, shinier skies, the tang
in the air, the great inevitable arrival.

We still read of it, the glorious season,
even though the celebrated flocks of birds
have long been absent above our cities.
We who live low can most likely glimpse it now,
if at all, from the window of a train.
The plains still demonstrate spring quite clearly.
These days, the storms that pass are so remote
they touch upon no more than our roof-top aerials.

Ulrike Draesner
Two Poems from 'synger med fuld styrke' on Bert Brecht and Ruth Berlau
Translated by Iain Galbraith

BB:

in the wood of tåsinge, alone/when it started to rain
November 1938

climbed the rise of ancient gleaming beeches
through the heaps of leaves the ground
so soft and steep the hill, we came here
once from islands too small you, blown in
from rabbit-land me. roosting in the trees
was this enormous flock of crows they too
great fat crows climbing in alarm i
almost slipped back down the slope. on top
then bushes and thorns a pasty pale white
field awash with mist. going down
was like skiing back . . . back home . . . those
shining branches in the wood to swing
on. again the field below with pheasants
sparring three. the woods seemed full
of fowl of gurgles calls and the trees
some 200 their silvery-smooth gristle
erect and taut in the mist a single being
surging on before as if i'd stepped into
a film, a slice of danish angst. it rained
and this was the border between two clouds

called exile one and exile two and i heard
plain to the invisible as rabbit-pie on these
yellow leaves snitch snatch hush the ferries fly
in the wood

RB:
svendborg song

summer 1939

little six-armed loudspeaker
hollyhock by the house . . .

july's ship is passing
silently by, two sails big, three small
lifeboat gleaming white
you sway over the Sound

little six-armed loudspeaker
hollyhock by the house . . .
the ship has passed us by
two sails big, three small
its body black and white
like our text

the only lifeboat
hung back even
the waves broke
as if to depart

little two-armed loudspeaker
the hollyhock by the house.

David Constantine

Berlin. 1990

When it was over, they raised their stalls in the ruins
Or laid an old army blanket on the dust
To sell off the badges, trophies, medals and orders
All the insignia and paraphernalia
Forty years of it. I watched the arrival of a capacious tourist
    bus
With darkened windows, like a three-storey limo
And out of it tumbled in white
The West. I remember one beauty
Who tottered in heels across the rubble to the sale
And posed against the wasteland
In a flag and a fur hat.
What chortles on the side of the cameras!
But the sellers were trying out their smiles
Like something they would have to get used to.

From: Quatrains for a *Primer of our Times*. After Brecht's *War Primer*. Supply your own images.

Epitaph
We pile here in the usual ratio
Of us to you. So numerous in death
None has a stone and script to lie beneath.
This cicatrice, this bulldozed trench must do.

Fact
The fact is, friend, we matter more than you.
One husband, lover, son, father of ours
Outweighs at least a hundred such of yours.
It's a fact of life, my friend – and of death too.

Image Unavailable
No photos yet of the mothers of Iraq
Thanking us for cluster bombs. Must be they lack
The gift of seeing through our Secretary's eyes
And cannot know a blessing in disguise.

Birth Pangs
The school fell on him and he crawled out blind,
His teacher's in there brained, but never mind:
You don't need brains to know or eyes to see
These are the birth pangs of democracy.

Bert Papenfuss
Two Poems
Translated by Andrew Duncan

Dear Eugen,

You have popped up as
a privileged arsehole with concubine,
country house and chauffeur, come on lip-synching,
spittle-licking, and lording it about, stalking
down town like a *Collected Works* on stilts.

Instead of friskily hopping around the yard,
biffing monocausality hard, showing didactics
the three-sided card, you taught dialectics
to stewpot flies and crawlers up the system.

In the beginning, theatre work was not an exchange of
    assets,
neither by the way a natural communication
between humans, in freed-up rhythms –
the goggle box was on its way.

Children of sadness kept a high profile,
State enterprises stagnated, the people
was looking down the barrel of its property – up till today:
'Help us out to make Office a better product!'

Screwed into shape, snagged in the official fishnet
one protects oneself with less wit,
as one administers reproofs
and smokes fat cigars.

Smoking is defence – 'there is nothing to follow'.
The 70-year family business of the estate
administering rights and leftovers
is, speaking tactfully . . .

The smugly benign licence to milk
those little things between humans is another blow.
'Another people' is of course no way out, either,
you had your nose blocked by your pince-nez!
yours, Bert

With all your might

Ignoring the fact
that I am not interested
in what doesn't interest me,
it does not interest me
what people know.
It can't amount to much.
What they think they know,
is only what they recognize,
and that inaccurately for the most part.
What interests me
is what people believe.
        With all their might
        and if you like with all their violence.

Ignoring the fact
that I am not interested
in what doesn't interest me,
what gets my interest going
is what people still believe in.
It can't amount to much.
Who carries it all on his back
should rear up and unload
what he hates, and keep, what suits him.
With a bit of basic science
you come to have a conscience.
       With all your might, individual protest,
       and if you like with all your violence.

On the contrary, ignoring the fact
that I am not interested
in what doesn't interest me,
what especially interests me
is what people steal.
They should whip away
what bureaucrats casually
allotted without justice.
Let court eunuchs ingest
what crawled out of their arses.
Property should remain in theft
       With all our might, mass stampede,
       and if you like with all our violence.

Albert Ostermaier
Two Poems
Translated by Tom Cheesman

offside trap or: brecht finds benn

you fail to understand how utterly isolated I am
here how I freeze like a ptolemaic sphere my mind
lacking any connection with my surroundings
sounds severe dear benn and self chosen but go
and watch a match for a small outlay get your
account of yourself unfrozen where the ground
rings with healthy outbreaks of feeling *oh*
those runs on eternity fitted into ninety minutes
of never just bone healing parapsychosis and
synchronised reeling you're exhibiting
melancholia again *you'd heave lager sagas of*
aster eaters choked by smoke bombs onto my
desktop you spread a lot of dense fog yourself
stop being such a prig soccer's disinhibiting
ach du z' trick-'-ling on flown extinguished sound
soccer teaches masses how to think in the mode of
potentiality *but this is thinking headed down the*
road to inanity let me buy you a pendulum header
frame some time saved from a life of crime now
he licks fat dripping chicken wings oh my sublime
that's morphology that's more fool you and your
august solitude at every moment the catastrophe
or a masterstroke are possible *that recalls my the*
late ego seceding self immortelle or feeding balls

down the wings cross into the box bicycle shot
there's a term I've not heard before tibulski tor
the lesson is things can be changed in seconds
which is more than history teaches *I feel only
emptiness* it's a practical class for revolutionaries
these feverishly stoked-up frenzies the path to pure
play always led through struggle *that way lies
muscle cramp ugly short trousers flesh on grass
just crass* but the one-twos and the songs that
they sing *passes me by* blue and white are the
colours of the sky *I'd have thought a line that
trite could only be by one of your mistresses but
no it's the terraces* and their ethereal sad sad
tralalas how about this we are the arminias take us
on and you'll see stars *I'd sing that my ars don't
make me think about their grim conurbation its
streets like urinals tomorrow it's the clinic* if
you want to reach the finals and win play the spin
system game the quick rotation *never did a new
life begin more sceptically coldly in less expectation
and if I were to join you whose would the point
be* only the blues *I see and then fate's symmetry
would guarantee that they'd never get laid again
yours is a beer* I love a good head *I'll get one in
for you and race back here from deep space* but
please no more spinning round and don't forget
the score dear benn the nil conceded must be
fought for

from: repeat
hollywood elegy

I
brittle tough sky the clouds are for
the angels to dab off their nail
varnish with aviation fuel pisses
down over the city and hell has
spread a couple more blocks
overnight in a rest home the
communists paint their dreams'
subtitles in big wobbly letters
on supermarket cardboard
& stretch arms out from their
wheelchairs as the traffic
builds on sunset sunshine
crashes off shades till eyes
weep quicksilver

The poems were commissioned by the South Bank
Centre, London, for Poetry International 2006.

Bertolt Brecht
Four new Herr Keuner Stories and a
Short Reflection on the Constitution
Translated by Tom Kuhn

The truth, his house, his car and his public – these were the things, Brecht complained, that the Nazis had stolen, and he wanted them back. The Herr Keuner stories, written mostly in exile over many years (from 1929 to 1949), were just one of the ways the writer sought to reassert himself and get his own back. Keuner (both a Bavarian *keiner*, or 'nobody', and a Greek *koinon*, 'the generality') is at the same time something of a self-projection and an oracle for modern times, a cunning, not infrequently devious, thinker, who attacks problems from unexpected angles and couches his infuriatingly inconsistent 'truths' in lapidary maxims. His *Gestus* and attitude are closely related to Brecht's theatre work; indeed the figure first crops up in the great *Fatzer* fragment (where he asks, 'Everything changes, but we/Should we not change?'), and a ghost of Herr K. even puts in an appearance in the first version of *Galileo* The first major German edition of some of the dozens of these short Keuner sketches, the *Kalendergeschichten* (Berlin, January 1949), was Brecht's first new publication, so to speak a visiting card, when he returned to the divided country after the war.

It seems extraordinary, in this fiftieth year since Brecht's death on 14 August 1956, to record that there is still so much by one of the twentieth century's leading writers that has not been published in English. It is not just a question of letters and notes, or drafts and variants of familiar works. More than half of Brecht's over 2300 poems have not been translated, or have not been published in translation (there is of course a problem here, in that the heirs and their gatekeeper, the German publisher Suhrkamp, have maintained strict control over publications), and there are substantial works in prose too, notably the *Flüchtlingsgespräche* (Refugee Conversations), something of a companion to the Keuner stories, which remain unknown to an English-speaking readership. In this anniversary year the rights to Brecht in English have passed, along with the whole of the drama backlist, from Methuen to A&C Black; and there is perhaps reason to hope for some renewed energy in Brecht publishing in Britain. Looking across to Germany, it is clear that Brecht is now, one might say 'at last', prized as one of that country's truly great cultural figures. The interest in the media has been more intense even than in 1998, the one hundredth anniversary of his birth. Brecht's star is in the ascendant.

That interest has been fuelled by two recent discoveries of previously unknown material. When the documentary film-maker Renata Mertens-Bertozzi died in Zurich in December 2000, several cartons (originally American coffee chests) full of Brecht manuscripts were discovered amongst her effects. Brecht had stayed with her in 1949, and she had acted as an assistant, translator and agent. It was treasure trove of unknown versions of familiar plays, theoretical writings, prose fragments and poems. Then, at the beginning of this anniversary year, an even more sensational collection was acquired by the Brecht Archive, again dating primarily from the American exile and those few months in Switzerland after the war. The trade-unionist Victor Cohen had then been a friend to the Brechts, a valued political discussant, and evidently an assiduous collector. Although he died in 1975, his own sons had no inkling of the extent of the collection until they had to clear out the cellar in the suburbs of Zurich, where they found 2500 sheets of Brecht manuscripts, typescripts, personal documents and letters. There is correspondence with Helene Weigel, Hanns Eisler, Christopher Isherwood and Charles Laughton amongst many others, there are notes on the genesis of *The Caucasian Chalk Circle*, and there is plentiful evidence to re-write the whole story of how Brecht planned his return to Europe and to the old country, exploiting every opportunity for new publications and for new theatre projects.

The following Herr Keuner stories come from the first of these remarkable finds, the Mertens-Bertozzi collection, which contained a whole folder of 58 'geschichten vom h k', many of them in several versions, and fifteen of them previously completely unknown. The *Tales from the Calendar* (i.e. a version of the original *Kalendergeschichten*), translated by Yvonne Kapp and Michael Hamburger, was published in the Methuen English-language Brecht edition in 1961, and a new selection of *Stories of Mr Keuner*, translated by Martin Chalmers, appeared in City Lights (San Francisco) in 2001, but there is no full English edition, and these four stories have never appeared anywhere in English before.

Music off the peg

One day, in front of a small audience, Herr Keuner sang two songs with more or less the same melody. People chided him. Either, they protested, the melody fits the first song, in which case it doesn't fit the second, or the other way around. It could only fit both if one of the poems were sufficient on its own and the other superfluous. Herr Keuner defended himself saying: 'Both my songs can be performed with more or less the same underlying gesture (which doesn't mean they are in competition, since the gesture is not the main thing, or if it is the main thing then it may have need of several songs), so the same or a similar melody will work. You can tailor clothes that suit a person so well that they wouldn't suit anyone who looks a bit different, but I don't like clothes like that. At best they will do for Sundays. Work clothes can be clothes off the peg.'

Herr Keuner and expression

Herr Keuner was so intolerant of people who were preoccupied with themselves that he even proposed that the *expression* of sadness or happiness should, if possible, be suppressed, so that the impression could not arise that someone was improperly occupied with their own affairs. 'How should I tell everyone the same story? Or be the same for everyone?' he said. 'I am not sad or happy for one and all.'

A student deserts Herr Keuner

One of Herr Keuner's students deserted him. He had enjoyed his company: there was no one whose opinion he more enjoyed contradicting. Nonetheless Herr Keuner was not downhearted. 'He was a good student,' he said, 'one of the best! It is a pity that he has left, but it is not a bad thing. It would be a very bad thing if *you* two left', and he pointed unabashed at two whom he did not particularly value, '*you* haven't learnt anything!'

The wine and the grapes

Herr Keuner was asked whether suffering doesn't make for a better person. He disagreed, saying: 'If the grapes were only there for the wine, then we should value the treading as highly as the Pope values Franco.'

Don't mention breaking the constitution!

Even after the Reichspresident had already committed his third breach of the constitution many Social Democrats still quietly warned one another not to mention it. Whatever you do don't mention it, they said anxiously, otherwise every inhibition against breaking the constitution will be gone. Once the people or the President learns that the constitution has already been broken no warnings will help. As it is, we can still warn against breaking the constitution. And, following this train of thought, they demonstrated by the sweat of their brows that, each time the constitution was broken, nothing untoward had happened. When it came about that there was no constitution left, there had still been no breach.

Gonçalo Tavares
Five stories
Translated by Desirée Jung

Gonçalo M. Tavares was born in 1970 and had his first publication in 2001. Since then, he has published fiction, poetry, short fiction and drama. He is the recipient of various awards, including the prestigious José Saramago in 2005 – the highest of its kind in the Portuguese language – for the fiction *Jerusalem*, which also won the Prize Millenium Ler/Círculo de Leitores in 2004, and other prizes too. Many of his books have been adapted into different media such as visual installations, theatre plays, films, in addition to being translated into many languages and countries: Spain, France, Brazil, Italy, Poland, India, etc.

One peculiar aspect of Gonçalo's publications is his habit of numbering and dividing all his books into series. The *Black Books*, for example, are part of the fiction series whose thematic focus is on the morality of human existence in war times; *Jerusalem* is an example. Another fascinating category, also part of the fiction genre, is the series of Gentlemen or Sirs, who, besides living in the same neighbourhood, all share the same oddity: of having names of famous writers, Calvino, Walser, Valéry, Brecht etc. The short stories or tales featured in these books are not only funny and playful but profound and exquisite. Mr.Brecht is one great character of this series and, like the many others, his favorite exercise is telling stories. And in his case, the stories are told in a 'brechtian' way, with wit and quickness, for a growing audience.

Um país agradável

Era um país muito agradável para viver, mas as pessoas eram tão preguiçosas que quando o presidente ordenou que defendessem as fronteiras, eles bocejaram. Foram invadidos.

Os invasores também começaram a ficar preguiçosos e, um dia, quando o novo presidente ordenou que os homens defendessem as fronteiras, todos bocejaram. Foram de novo invadidos. Agora por homens vindo de um outro país.

Mais uma vez os invasores em pouco tempo ficaram preguiçosos, e quando pela terceira vez um novo presidente ordenou que os homens defendessem as fronteiras, todos bocejaram. Mais uma vez foram invadidos. O país estava cada vez mais populoso.

Tal repetiu-se até que todos os povos – mesmo os que vinham do outro lado do globo – haviam já invadido aquele país, e depois, sucessivamente, sido invadidos. Já não havia gente em mais lado nenhum: concentravam-se todos naquele país agradável.

Foi nesta altura que o novo presidente ordenou a invasão do resto do mundo pois o mundo estava completamente vazio – à sua mercê, portanto. Porém, todos os homens bocejaram.

E então ele (sem o notar) avançou, sozinho.

A nice country

It was a very nice country to live in, yet people were so lazy that when the president ordered them to defend the borders, they yawned. They were invaded.

The invaders also began to feel lazy and, one day, when the new president ordered his men to defend the borders, they all yawned. They were invaded again. This time by men coming from another country.

Before long, the invaders once again became lazy, and when, for the third time, a new president ordered his men to defend the borders, all of them yawned. Once again they were invaded. The country became more and more crowded.

This was repeated until every nation – even those who had come from the other side of the globe – had already invaded that country, and later, one after another, had themselves been invaded. There weren't any people left anywhere else: they were all concentrated in that one nice country.

It was at this point that the new president ordered the invasion of the rest of the world, because the world was completely empty – and, for this reason, at his mercy. Still, all the men yawned.

And then (unnoticed) he moved on, alone.

O desempregado com filhos

Disseram-lhe: só te oferecemos emprego se te cortarmos a mão.
Ele estava desempregado há muito tempo; tinha filhos, aceitou.
Mais tarde foi despedido e de novo procurou emprego.
Disseram-lhe: só te oferecemos emprego se te cortarmos a mão que te resta.
Ele estava desempregado há muito tempo; tinha filhos, aceitou.
Mais tarde foi despedido e de novo procurou emprego.
Disseram-lhe: só te oferecemos emprego se te cortarmos a cabeça.
Ele estava desempregado há muito tempo; tinha filhos, aceitou.

Unemployed with children

They told him: we can only offer you a job if we cut off your hand.
He'd been unemployed for a long time; he had children, he accepted.
Later on he was fired and again he began looking for a job.
They told him: we can only offer you a job if we cut off your other hand.
He'd been unemployed for a long time; he had children, he accepted.
Later on he was fired and again he began to look for a job.
They told him: we can only offer you a job if we cut off your head.
He'd been unemployed for a long time; he had children, he accepted.

O cantor

Um pássaro foi atingido com um tiro na asa direita e passou por isso a voar na diagonal.

Mais tarde foi atingido na asa esquerda e viu-se obrigado a deixar de voar, utilizando apenas as duas patas para andar no chão.

Mais tarde foi atingido por uma bala na pata esquerda e passou por isso a andar na diagonal.

Uma outra bala atingiu-o, semanas depois, na pata direita, e o pássaro deixou de poder andar.

A partir desse momento dedicou-se às canções.

The singer

A bird was shot in its right wing and then began to fly diagonally.

Later, it was hit in the left wing and had to give up flying, using only its two feet to walk on the ground.

Later, it was hit by a bullet in the left foot and then began to walk diagonally.

Weeks later, another bullet hit it in the right foot, and the bird was no longer able to walk.

From that moment on, it devoted itself to song.

Torcicolo

A mulher do Rei, que gostava de passear pelo reino a ver
como iam as coisas, um certo dia fez um pequeno torcicolo no
pescoço que a impedia de rodar a cabeça. Como o pescoço da
Rainha não melhorava o Rei ordenou que todo o país começasse
a funcionar em trajectórias circulares à frente da varanda do
palácio.

Stiff Neck

The wife of the King, who liked to go for a stroll through
the Kingdom to see how things were going, twisted her neck,
which prevented her from moving her head. Since the Queen's
neck wouldn't get better, the King ordered that the whole
country begin to function in circular trajectories in front of the
palace's balcony.

O gatinho

Havia um gato que todos os fins de tarde se aproximava do
dono e lhe lambia os sapatos com a sua língua minúscula.

Vencendo uma certa timidez e uma certa precaução
higiénica, o homem um dia decidiu descalçar-se para observar
se o gato lhe lambia os pés como fazia aos sapatos.

Foi aí que o tigre, que se disfarçara de gato durante anos,
decidiu que era o seu momento, e em vez de lamber, comeu.

The kitty

There was a cat who every late afternoon approached its owner and licked his shoes with its tiny tongue.

Overcoming a certain shyness, and a certain hygienic caution, the man decided one day to strip off his shoes and observe if the cat licked his feet as it did his shoes.

It was then that the tiger, which had been disguised as a cat for years, decided that his moment had come, and instead of licking, he ate.

Thomas Brasch
Five poems
Translated by Ken Cockburn

Thomas Brasch was born in Yorkshire in 1945, the son of
Jewish anti-fascists who had emigrated from Nazi Germany.
The family settled in the German Democratic Republic, and
his father made a successful career within the ruling Socialist
Unity Party. Brasch attended an army school, but did not
follow a military career. A protest over the 1968 Soviet
invasion of Czechoslovakia led to a prison term. He worked for
a time with Helene Weigel in the Brecht Archive, before
becoming a freelance writer in East Berlin. Following the
expatriation of Wolf Biermann in late 1976, he moved to West
Berlin with his partner, the actress Katharina Thalbach, and
their daughter. Initially feted in the west, as a playwright,
poet, short story writer and film-maker, his later writing career
focused on Shakespeare adaptations, and a huge novel about
the murderer Karl Brunke – 14,000 pages in manuscript,
reputedly – only a fraction of which was ever published, as a
novella in 1999. He died of heart failure in 2001. A book of
uncollected and unpublished poems *Wer durch mein Leben will*
was published posthumously in 2002.

'Einstein's Embankment' and 'The Amicable Hosts' are taken from *Der schöne 27. September (The Glorious 27ᵗʰ September)*, a collection of poems which was a great success on its appearance in 1980; a new edition was issued in 2004. '. . . and Practice' and 'An End' are taken from *Rotter und weiter* (1978), which contains the script of the play *Rotter*, premiered in Stuttgart in late 1977, with additional texts such as these, contextualising the play. 'Historical Translation' is from 'Der Papiertiger' ('The Paper Tiger', 1976), a performance script consisting of a sequence of seventeen poems.

. . . and Practice

The world has been changed, shout the prisoners.
Freed from their enemies' jails, they enter
the Government palace
and issue directives.

Up on the tops the climber sees
a new world, but in the valley the peasants see
the same old mountain.
Has it been levelled because from the summit
the climber no longer sees it?

Now we are in power, they say and
try things out from their new positions.
We're the same as we were in the old days, but
our work is different. Not baskets of food,
instead we now distribute
medals, so
the world has been changed.

Dwarves, shout the climbers into the valley.
Dwarves, the peasants shout back, creeping away
to their houses as another avalanche crashes down.

A fresh avalanche, from the same old mountain.

An End

He has not stopped her. She
has climbed over the stone. She
has not fallen and has not looked up at him. She
has left him.

When he awoke and saw
how she pulled her dress over her thin body,
when he saw how she took her stockings from the chair,
how she grasped the handle, he knew:

I have not stopped her. Her journey
has not found its end in me. I have not quenched
her thirst. I have not taken her fear away.
I was for her not enough.

Historical Translation

This a woman says to you:
You should have been the first we expelled. You
had already betrayed us when you crawled all over Fulvia
for the first time, when you spoke of grand sums of money
for the first time, so as to part her thighs
a second time.

This a woman says to you:
I should have struck you down when you still
lay limp in Fulvia's bed and were telling her
about Catalina's grand scheme and your bravery,
so as to hide your weakness behind grand words.
Come away from the window, Curius. In every landscape
it is your own face that you see.

This a woman says to you all:
I have seen children at my breast, who
on the street were called men. I have
heard men betray official secrets, once
their testicles were empty.
Come away from the window, Curius.
Now we are spent.Now Cicero has us surrounded.
What is there still to see beyond the window, Curius.

At last. Strike him down.

Einstein's Embankment
(Heroin)

1
The needle into
one's own flesh: behind
the toilet-door take leave of
a state: it is by all good spirits taken leave of.

2
I saw Nakry my untrue love
(it wasn't mentioned) at Einstein Embankment her teeth
were rotten her nails black, aged
ten years in two. I
gave her no money, although
she wanted no money.

3
Into the blood, the dream
into the brain, the dream, as far as it can
the shrouds are stiff
your blood is drying in my hand

4
Between opposition and acquisition,
she says, living is unsound.
I shoot, the policeman on patrol shoots too.
The difference, she says, is well-founded.

5
You did not recognise me: That
is good. My skin is grey. I
have achieved my goal: I am
unusable.

6
Her hands are shaking. What
she has before her is
death. What she has behind her was
not a life.

7
What did you dream of this night now past
I dreamt of nothing in the night now past
Who made yesterday evening their last
I don't know, someone perhaps made it her last

The Amicable Hosts

They invite me to a meal.
They push my chair in at the table.
They shove a spoon into my mouth.
They press a pencil into my hand.
They say YOU CAN START and turn away:
Everyone has the tool
that they deserve.

Mimi Khalvati
Five Ghazals

Englishing the Ghazal

Agha Shahid Ali, the late Kashmiri-American poet who did so much to familiarise American poets with the ghazal, asked himself, while translating Faiz, if he 'could make English behave outside its aesthetic habits'. Faced with the same question, I am particularly challenged by the very aspects of the canonical ghazal which seem to contradict our aesthetic criteria for writing poetry.

The form itself is difficult enough: the monorhyme (*qafiya*), the refrain (*radif*) and, most alarmingly, the final 'signature couplet' which requires the author to mention him/herself by name or pseudonym. But how to use the form without the stratagems of disguise we expect in contemporary formal poetry? Using strict and fully audible rhyme; gratifying the reader's expectation instead of subverting it; employing a syntax that invites the audience to 'join in' the refrain, much like the 'hook' in song lyrics; avoiding, in the absence of enjambment, metrical monotony – these are some of the technical challenges.

But thematically, there is the 'disunity' of the ghazal, in which couplets move around on a lateral plane – from the

personal to the political, the meditative to the satiric – rather
than in a linear, sequential line of logic, with only the rhyme
and refrain to act as binding. This is still beyond me. Then
there is the perilous question of cliché. Translating an aesthetic
in which images are relished less for their quiddity than for
their emblematic power, using a diction that is colloquial but
also aphoristic or rhapsodic – how can I do this in English
without being corny? More dubious still, how can I, a woman
poet, address the Beloved from a submissive, even subservient,
position, without irony, and call myself a feminist?

I remember a very old and well-thumbed copy of Hafez an
Iranian friend showed me, interleaved with countless post-it
notes in varying shades of yellow. These, she explained, marked
the many occasions in her life when she had consulted Hafez, as
one would the I Ching, on their auspices. Her life and Hafez's
ghazals were forever inextricably linked. Mine, without my
mother tongue, forever diminished. I long to english the
ghazal and do what I might do if I were writing in my first
language.

Ghazal: It's Heartache

When you wake to jitters every day, it's heartache.
Ignore it, explore it, either way, it's heartache.

Youth's a map you can never refold,
from Yokohama to Hudson Bay, it's heartache.

Ah love, love, who are centuries old,
it's not time or absence I can't weigh, it's heartache.

Heartache with women, heartache with men,
call myself straight, unexpectedly gay, it's heartache.

Follow the piper, lost on the road,
whistle the tune that led him astray: it's heartache.

Stop at the roadside, name each flower,
the loveliness that will always stay: it's heartache.

Why do nightingales sing in the dark?
Ask the *radif*, it will only say 'it's heartache'.

Let *khalvati*, a 'quiet retreat',
close my ghazal and heal as it may its heartache.

Ghazal: To hold me

I want to be held. I want somebody dear to hold me
in the wind and the rain when nobody's near to hold me.

I want to be touched as the tree touches sky
and sky touches earth so horizons appear to hold me.

I want to strike out as a flock strikes for home
and home is now this, now that, warm hemisphere to hold
    me.

I want to uncoil a long river of hair,
my beloved to sleep, to cross sleep's frontier to hold me.

I want all that has been denied me. And more.
Much more than God in some lonely stratosphere to hold
    me.

I want hand and eye, sweet roving things, and land
for grazing, praising, and the last pioneer to hold me.

I want my ship to come in, hopes to run high
before my back's so bowed even children fear to hold me.

I want to die being held. Hearing my name
thrown, thrown like a rope from a very old pier to hold me.

I want to catch the last echoes, reel them in
like a curing-song in the creel of my ear to hold me.

I want Rodolfo to sing, flooding the gods,
Ah Mimi! as if I were her and he, here, to hold me.

Ghazal: My Son

He's wearing a red silk shirt, my son.
He's done me a dreadful hurt, my son.

Now that the devil has shown his face,
he's hiding under my skirt, my son.

A mother is earth, but earth is sick.
A mother's nothing but dirt, my son.

The floor of the gym is strewn with limbs.
Children are lying inert, my son.

I see lights, he says, *hear voices too!*
Obscenities to pervert my son.

Don't look at the lights, the voice is yours.
What can I say to alert my son?

Don't look at the world, a beast that kills,
a savage you can't convert, my son?

What's happened to trust? Don't screen your eyes,
green eyes you always avert, my son.

White roses are heaped on children's graves
while I, even I, desert my son.

Ghazal: Lilies of the Valley

Everywhere we walked we saw lilies of the valley.
Every time we stopped were more lilies of the valley.

Umbrellas passed – fathers, sons,
holding out a hand that bore lilies of the valley.

Every citizen of France
bearing through his own front door lilies of the valley.

But we were out of the know,
though reluctant to ignore lilies of the valley.

Our first May Day in Paris,
knowing nothing of folklore lilies of the valley.

Of Jenny Cook and Chabrol's
famous buttonhole that wore lilies of the valley.

He who sang *Viens poupoule, viens!*
and started the fashion for lilies of the valley.

How fashion then conferred, free
on *les ouvriers* at Dior, lilies of the valley.

What did we know, our luck know,
of charmed *muguets des bois* or lilies of the valley?

And though I wore the perfume
I have always worn before – lilies of the valley

– Diorissimo that is,
no one whispered, 'Meem, *j'adore* lilies of the valley'.

No one made false promises.
And if they did, who blames poor lilies of the valley?

Ghazal: The Candles of the Chestnut Trees

I pictured them in the dark at night –
            the candles of the chestnut trees.
Their name alone made them self-ignite –
            the candles of the chestnut trees.

I pictured them in the pouring rain
as they really are, pink-tinged on white –
            the candles of the chestnut trees.

How many there are and each the same!
same shape and colour, angle, height –
            the candles of the chestnut trees.

Seen from below, most unseen,
they throw no shadow, cast no light –
            the candles of the chestnut trees.

I saw how distance matters more
than nearness, clearness, to see upright
            the candles of the chestnut trees.

Inspired by *Christ the apple tree**,
I looked for a figure to recite
            the candles of the chestnut trees.

Lacking faith, I could do no more
than find a refrain to underwrite
            the candles of the chestnut trees.

*18th-century American folk hymn

As May drew on, the more I saw,
the more they lost that first delight –
                    the candles of the chestnut trees.

I've searched for sameness all my life
but Mimi, nothing's the same despite
                    the candles of the chestnut trees.

Damian Walford Davies
'Kilvert'
With illustrations by Lucy Wilkinson

I came late to the famous diary of Francis Kilvert (1840–79). Published 1938–40, it was immediately acknowledged by readers as a classic. Valued for its detailed observations of nature and social life, it is an important social document; it is also resonantly lyrical. I found it disturbing. Kilvert's brilliant writing betrays a fascination with the darker side of rural life, and the entries are charged with suppressed desire. The borderland location of Clyro, Radnorshire, amplifies the oddnesses recorded. I was drawn to these vignettes. Something in the writing suggested the need for amplification, and the 'Kilvert' sequence enters into dialogue with its subject, responding to short quotations from the diary with poems that both extend and crystallise. (Two other so-called *ekphrastic* enterprises come to mind: Geoffrey Hill's response to lines from Cesare Pavese's diary in *Without Title*, and R. S. Thomas's *The Echoes Return Slow*, in which autobiographical poems and prose pieces fascinatingly play off each other.) I chose entries that worried me; they sit above the poems as both epigraphs and epitaphs. The poems function as a 'commentary' – replying, excavating, developing. I aimed for a spareness of language in tune with

Kilvert's economy. The voice shifts, and the line-breaks are meant to cut open and reveal – which, I hope, adds to the strangeness of the portraits of barely contained desire (numbers 2, 4, 5, 6, 9), violence (4, 5, 10, 12), madness and death (2, 3, 7, 11).

1.
The baby was baptised in ice which was broken and swimming
about in the font.

There was awkward-
ness, but he broke ice-
crust delicately as a
brûlée;
        these, he said, the sweet
shards and bergs
that save our souls.

2.
At Rhos Goch Lane House no one was at home so I stuck an ivy leaf
into the latch hole.

Improvised, so
you'd know I'd been:
a dying trefoil calling-
card, my meaning
veined on green
vellum pushed
into interior space.

When you come
in, press it between your
pages so it stains.

3.

Her pretty portrait still on the dining room mantelpiece . . . On the
bookshelves stood two cases of stuffed birds . . .

He thought they'd please
her. She thought it
cruel, that embarrassment
of birds, that parliament
of fowls between Hansard
and Hazlitt, posed
passerine, wired for flight.

     So early dead,
she said that one close
day she heard them cry for
air in the evacuated cases.

4.

It was the first time I had seen clergyman's daughters helping to
castrate lambs . . . they carried it off uncommonly well.

They held them like cellos,
the kneeling hands
bent to their relieving
work. It was
wrong all round. Still,

they played beautifully,
drawing something like
music from the bleating
between their legs.

5.
Very hot in morning Church, and an enormous bumble bee crawled over the white cloth . . .

      Tiger-
striped furzeball, louche
half-ounce of real
presence, had him bum-
bling through the

service, half wishing
it would sting
through each faint
dress.

6.
An angel satyr walks these hills.

Here between –
admiring cloud forms,
fancying the faster
parodies of shadow.

Here –
between the up-
lands' candour and the
valley's petty cleavages.

Now chaste,
now chafing at the collar.

7.
While I waited in the kitchen the low deep voice upstairs began
calling, 'Murder! John Lloyd! John Lloyd! Murder!'

Mrs Watkins dies
like clockwork
every day at three;
her grim chiasmus
ringing out across
the farm, bringing

in her son from
carrying oats, fresh-
pressed linen
in his arms.

8.
The stories about the baboon of Maesllwch Castle grow more and
more extraordinary.

More lord than pet –
parvenu, debouching
from the shadows
like some mad déb
down the dog-
leg balusters.

Last week it made a bee-
line for the Captain's
tails and Lady Burrell's
furs, its coat of arms that
crass heraldic derrière.

9.

*. . . on dark nights, the gentlemen pulled out the tails of their shirts
and walked before to show the way and light the ladies.*

The 'Dursley Lanterns' –
dapper will-o'-the-wisps
in lanes around great
houses; the phosphor-
escence of pressed Irish
linen moving in
        England's dark.

For every Jill a jack-
o'-lantern, a suit of lights –

    and beneath the starched
swagger of those tails
the luminous flesh-
light lanterns of the bodies.

10.

*. . . the bag fox had been kept in a dark cellar so long that he was
dazed and half blind when he was turned out.*

It must have hurt like
the taste of metal
as it woke to serrations of
light, the aperture

widening suddenly
into blindness.

It left the sack
flaccid, cooling, like
flayed skin

11.

All the time we were in the tunnel these lighted matches were
travelling from hand to hand in the darkness.

The Box Tunnel pashed
the chatter, snuffed
the Flower-Show hats.
Against the black someone
struck a brim-
stone match. It passed
from man to woman like
a sacrament, hands
touching without meaning
to
          Later, among the flowers,
he recalled the Clyro tales
of corpse candles moving
in the dark.

12.

. . . the young Bryants held him down in the furrow and ploughed
him into the ground.

He was a bad seed,
the sod, refused to lie
still as the plough-
knife skinned the clods.

But they sowed
Robert Jefferies deep
to see whether
his curly crop would
blossom into
          something better.

Ellen Coverdale
Two Poems

Lorenzetti's *Last Supper*

Black outside but for a few bright specks
Of redundant universe, the room itself
Lit by haloes and the Christ feeds
The dead star Judas
His lines. It is storytime, they are sitting uncomfortably
On marble sepulchres. Much cosier
Is the cramped kitchen
Next door
With a roaring fire
And the cat lies in a dozy heaven of warmth
And the dog is licking the leavings off the platters of the
    important people
And a couple of scullions are flirting and nattering.

So there always was and is still
Life
And in a room next door the Leader among his men
Big with ideas. Alas for you
Life, the son God hurled
At the earth like an asteroid
And marked the place of impact with a massacre
Will be leaving shortly in darkness at noon
On his long trajectory
Threading suicide, martyrdom, supernovae of killing.

L'Origine du monde
(after Courbet)

Oh, I forgot,
She said, the rest's
Incognita
And pulled the sheet
Of map up over her
Becoming then
Above the waist
Mare Nostrum
Crossing her heart
Under the caves
Of Thetis and through
The river of Leda
Smiling invisibly

And leaving him
Between the slopes
From hip to knee
And knee to her
Magenta-painted toes
Still deepening
His study of
The intricately
Lipped and lobed
And hooded nest
And den of origins

And seeing all
He saw there shown
As though he showed
Or murmured it
To her: a streaming
Scalded head
Of land raised up
By fire through the sea
Acropolis
And terraces
That overflowed
In scalloped pools
Of lupin blue
And we were there
The pair of us
The strollers through
The asphodels
For centuries
He said she said
And if again
By fire and ice
The sea is raised
The land sunk down
We'll grow our gills

Again, she said
And join the fish
The nosy fish
The warm and smiling
Suckling fish
Who know our kind
Of old, who've seen
Us tesseraed
On rippling floors
And red on black
On fired bowls
In the sealed holds
Of foundered ships.

My dabbler
My just begun
Enquire me more
Deepen me
There's more and more
Under the sea
The Middle Sea
Whose centrique part
Sends circles out
That break upon
The shores around
And tremor through
The sands and snows
There's more and more
I promise you
Crossing my heart
Under the sea
And smiling through.

Pascale Petit
Two Poems

I trained at the Royal College of Art and worked as a sculptor before turning to poetry full-time, so it's natural to me to draw from the visual arts for imagery. I have written a series of poems in the voice of Frida Kahlo, *The Wounded Deer*, and these may appear in a full-length book, *The Thorn Necklace,* with the paintings in 2007/8. I also have a sequence in the voice of Franz Marc, where I've juxtaposed his innocent-horse paintings with his last days at Verdun – art with war.

I wrote these two poems when I was preparing to tutor a poetry course at Tate Modern this summer, in the new Poetry and Dream wing. As I wanted students to write poems sparked by the surrealist art there, I thought I'd first try some out myself. I decided Magritte's haunting reckless sleeper was my dead father. The objects embedded in the space beneath his coffin-alcove instantly became significant for me. I had not seen Leonor Fini's painting 'Little Hermit Sphinx' before. I peered past the feral sphinx-girl, into the dark hovel, which I identified as my mother's home where I'd lived as a teenager. I'd researched feral children and this seemed to be a feral family. If so, my mad mother was inside – terrifying and vulnerable.

The Reckless Sleeper
after René Magritte

You are lying in your alcove
with six treasures I buried with you –

a hand-mirror, a lit candle, a black hat,
an apple, a living bird and Maman's blue bow.

Wood grain surrounds you like
waves of REM dreaming.

The bow still smells of the evening
when you forced your hot candle

into the trembling bird in her thighs.
The apple turns its unbitten cheek

towards me. The mirror also turns its back
as if to hide its face. The bowler

is the one she wore to marry you
in a man's funeral suit. You sleep on,

Papa, but the dream never changes.

Little Hermit Sphinx
after a painting by Leonor Fini

The time to let me in has passed.
I am your little sphinx now –

your feral child. Tomorrow
I will run away to the woods

and live like a hermit. While
I've been sitting on the doorstep

I've caught a crow, hung
its heart from the lintel. Every hour

the door opens and your face glows
like a mirror struck by lightning.

You sit on your scorched chair
while the rain tears at me with claws.

You hold out your hand and show me
the source of thunder. Then

the door slams and I'm shut out again.
The sun probes the dark like a torch

and the forest mocks me.
Every tree shakes with laughter.

Jeff Nosbaum
'Ukiyo-e', after Ryoi

Note

Ukiyo ('the floating world') was originally a Buddhist term for the transience and unreality of material existence. The term gradually came to be used for the lifestyle of wealthy pleasure-seekers in 17th-century Edo (now Tokyo), and the woodblock prints of life in Edo that were popular among this milieu became known as ukiyo-e, 'images of the floating world'. Over the course of the 18th and early 19th centuries landscape prints by artists such as Hiroshige and Hokusai became a defining feature of ukiyo-e.

I first came across these landscape prints at an exhibition in the National Museum and Gallery of Wales in 2001, where the exhibition was prefaced by a definition of the floating world by the 17th-century Japanese writer Asai Ryoi, and this quote seemed to me to be a poem in waiting.

Ukiyo-e
after Ryoi

Turning our full attention
to the pleasures of the moon,
the snow, the cherry blossom
and the maple leaves;
singing, drinking wine, diverting
ourselves   in merely floating,

       we,
           upon the bridge,
           stare down, see only
the sun at the ripples, the glint
of light a sugared glaze; a gourd
is carried along with the river current:
                      this
is what we call the floating world.

Alison Brackenbury
'1.15 a.m.'

After-Images: the poem's secret life
A note on '1.15 a.m.'

I have spent years in quiet flight from my early notions of images. Poetry, I decided, lived in sound. But where were its echoes, its after-life? I was happy to see my poems wriggle under the poetry fence, but longed for a badger collar to track them into their new world.

Increasingly, this world became the Internet; disconcertingly, the poems drawn into its orbit veered towards the visual. When the editor of an online magazine accepted a poem about a play, he would paste a picture of an actress next to it, narrowing its words to fit her small mouth. The illicit borrowers of poems were bolder still. A poem about a pony shrank, shadowed by a photograph of a huge Friesian stallion. A poem I found full of pain appeared amongst the pastels of a designer's site, because it included the word 'pink'.

But the strangest re-vision swam before me in the early hours of the morning, on a Spanish site. (My Spanish is as fragmentary as my grasp of post-modernism.) There was one of my jauntier love-poems, ex-*TLS*, still in English, still punctiliously credited to me. But – it seemed – it was surrounded by the biography of an imaginary writer who shared my surname and place of birth.

The poem's proper freedom did not, I felt, include delivering my doppelgänger on a blue screen. I tried to detach myself from this story with another poem. But the Spanish site, complete with my poem, insinuated itself into the new poem, as I remembered the Moorish gardens of Majorca, with their cool walks out of January's blaze. After my long flight from images, I was back, through sleep and screens and Spain, with the after-image of the inner eye: this poem.

1.15 a m

I need sleep. I stare at a computer screen
I found by chance; a poem I wrote, my name;
Around it, a sea of Spanish. Strange
How you understand Spanish then not, like a clouding
   moon.
It features a writer, my birthplace. He wrote
The White City, a novel. A joke, I think, mad,
I type no novels. I will go
By marble walls, from roaring sun,
Sleep; till the world's computer screens
Drop to blue petals, one by one.

Tara Bergin
'Himalayan Balsam for a Soldier', after Christina Rossetti's 'Winter: My Secret'

Note

'I cannot ope to every one who taps'
Reading Christina Rossetti.

I had been working for some months on a poem about the wild riverbank flower that when touched, opens back its sides and flings its seeds out violently. Christina Rossetti's 'Winter: My Secret' interested me with its atmosphere of invasion and invitation. Her female speaker seems to be two things. She is an everyday woman wrapped up against the cold and she is also a thing of nature with a sensual and violent energy in her. Reading her, I feel that she is like those stage ghosts that the audience can see but the characters in the play cannot. She keeps moving objects about, to their confusion and alarm. Is she desperately trying to communicate, or is she just teasing and playing a sophisticated game? There is an ambiguity to her touch-me, touch-me-not talk. Her self may or may not be worth finding out about. Is she flaunting or hiding the inside of her flower? There is in Rossetti a superficially simple language which means that the form is not rare yet the content is startling, evocative, and essential. My poem was very much influenced by Rossetti's use of irony and ambivalence to create a disturbing mixture of carefreeness and intense concentration on the part of the speaker.

Christina Rossetti
Winter: My Secret

I tell my secret? No indeed, not I:
Perhaps some day, who knows?
But not today; it froze, and blows and snows,
And you're too curious: fie!
You want to hear it? well:
Only, my secret's mine, and I won't tell.

Or, after all, perhaps there's none:
Suppose there is no secret after all,
But only just my fun.
Today's a nipping day, a biting day;
In which one wants a shawl,
A veil, a cloak, and other wraps:
I cannot ope to every one who taps,
And let the draughts come whistling thro' my hall;
Come bounding and surrounding me,
Come buffeting, astounding me,
Nipping and clipping thro' my wraps and all.
I wear my mask for warmth: who ever shows
His nose to Russian snows
To be pecked at by every wind that blows?
You would not peck? I thank you for good will,
Believe, but leave the truth untested still.

Spring's an expansive time: yet I don't trust
March with its peck of dust,
Nor April with its rainbow-crowned brief showers,
Nor even May, whose flowers
One frost may wither thro' the sunless hours.

Perhaps some languid summer day,
When drowsy birds sing less and less,
And golden fruit is ripening to excess,
If there's not too much sun nor too much cloud,
And the warm wind is neither still nor loud,
Perhaps my secret I may say,
Or you may guess.

Himalayan Balsam for a Soldier

They don't see me but I walk
into Fitzgeralds with them the half-wounded,
I sit in there at the high table with my pint,
half-wounded, thinking, I will drag my
wounds in here.
I drag myself in and up to the high stool
among the guys with one arm and they
don't see me.
Here is your talisman I say, I whisper
hold it in your good hand and sing one
of your songs for me.
How does it go? Oh how does it go again?
There is blood on my hand, la la,
there is blood on my hand, la la.
Your talisman, I say, a foul flower.
Hold it in your hand and how full your good
hand will be with the
exploding.

Oliver Reynolds
MVM

'MVM' attempts to mix, in roughly equal proportions, versions of Martial with latter-day variations on similar themes. It was written five years ago and its original aims are now forgotten. However, its moods and methods, and the Latin example behind them, suggest certain features formed the basis of that attraction across distance which leads to translation.

City-life experienced as the press of bodies; the urban onlooker with his motes of pride and beams of prickliness; the trump-cards of money and sex: these are some of Martial's subjects. His style – pithy, knowing, obscene – construes itself as an argument: the lyrical impulse only escapes from corporeal existence fleetingly. (The constant star-gazer must be avoiding something under his nose.)

Though Martial's subject-matter and methods have perennial appeal, his compression of the elevated and vulgar may still cause offence. But the edge of offence is something that needs re-honing generation by generation. (One index of the limited scope of much contemporary verse is its inoffensiveness.) Martial is as good a whetstone as any.

MVM

These lines
Commemorate
Marcus Valerius Martial
To Whom
All Rome
Was partial
He lived
On pith and zest
Died cursing
And leaves us blessed

Each word a brick
each line a street
your city now
stands on its own

the slow river
swinging her skirts
the noise and soot
softened by rain

*

Rugger-bugger roaring from the showers:
Big Jim's doffed his jockstrap.

*

Juvenal
and Johnson
walk together

as Latin nouns
land on the Thames
one by one.

The shadows
are different,
but not the sun.

*

Leaving the clap clinic,
he tried to walk tall:
would she still love him,
(genital) warts and all?

*

The editor's poems are never seen
in this small well-funded magazine.
Let's give credit where credit's due.
He won't publish himself. Would you?

*

She gave me the anorexic volume
on Richmond Bridge:
        her own.

It was all I could do
not to give it
        a dip.

*

My bed (I wish! my mattress rather):
    fucked;
my sagging crumb-filled armchair:
    fucked;
so no surprise about my back:
    fucked.

                        *

One of the things that gets to you
    about being poor
is pubic hairs – other people's pubic hairs
    on the bathroom floor.

                        *

        Marble-dust
        grizzles the furrows
        of a field in Kent;

        fallen columns
        are wound
        with longweed;

        this is good: ruins
        are the only home
        the gods now have.

                        *

Tom takes it up the arse with shouts of laughter,
    but cries, after.

Why? It's a copper-bottomed fact
    he just loves being fucked.

So which is it: shame before his lover
    or sadness it's over?

                    *

        Lover-boy's cock
        giving him grief
        and the sad state
        of your sphincter –

        well, working out
        who has done what
        hardly requires
        Hercule Poirot.

                    *

The sweet acres of woodland are all yours,
    ditto the Chippendale and Spode.
Yours is the only key to the cellars –
    those rare vintages rarely shared.

But your private bedroom's flushed full-length Klimt
    by speaking just the once
could tell what we all know (you alone don't):
    your wife is anyone's.

                    *

The slow pruner
picks a last grape.
Trajan's schooner
has cleared the Cape.
Gilding the stern,
her torches burn.

Martial, in Spain,
has earned this drink.
Outside, harsh rain;
inside, dried ink.
Built in a day,
these lines will stay.

*

Closer than swans to the Thames
or the lily to its pad
closer than vines to the elm
　　is she to him
　　the night they wed

Closer than waves to the shore
or swoop of swifts to the road
closer than rain in the air
　　is he to her
　　the night they wed

Closer than dew to the leaf
or blossom tipping each bud
closer than bees to the hive
　　are both to love
　　the night they wed

*

The cold Hippodrome crowd
    are all in white
except for Horatius
    whose cloak is black.

He smirches the white ranks:
    plebeian cloth;
senatorial silks;
    Nero's ermine.

All watch sudden snow lap
    the chariots.
When it clears, Horatius
    is cloaked in white.

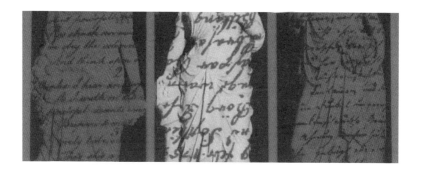

David Hart
'He came mute . . .'

This is a poem of a kind I find I write from time to time, as if translating from something almost known. Kafka in his letters and diaries locates such disjunctive moments; and I find those edge-of-almost-understanding moments, too, in Celan. At the edge of my understanding, too, and requiring translation are the fragments of poems Donald Crowhurst wrote when he started to falsify his log in the single-handed round-the-world race (as told by Nicholas Tomalin and Ron Hall in 'The strange voyage of Donald Crowhurst', 1970). And I have been listening to Syd Barrett's songs (as a member of Pink Floyd and on his own, who died recently after most of his life, as has been said, 'as a hermit'). Or perhaps in all of this sometimes it is understanding *too well* and very frightened. Perhaps Jacob demanding to know the ghostly stranger's name, with whom he fights, is a precursor.

He came mute with a message tied around his sore neck
in a language – we supposed a language – none of us here
could read, and he fell down dead then at our shoed feet.

So we buried him naked as naked he had come to us,
and we debated how to translate the note tied to him.
This work wearied us and we fell into a long, deep sleep.

We woke from a shared dream: a man stood speaking
on the steps of an important building while a woman
a distance away in long grass very quietly sang.

Where we were was all breeze now and we agreed:
trust this slight and insistent brush of air beating us
as it seemed beating us towards *somewhere* and we went.

I am alone now. We interpreted the breeze each in our
own very different way. Who has the untranslatable note?
Has anyone found the clue to it? There is a door open here

to a room that no longer exists in a building that no longer
exists where grass is dry and I want to pray. And I want tea
                                          and I want to
be held and to know. I ache as I think a lame bird aches.

Andrea Zanzotto
Hypersonnet
Translated by Peter Hainsworth

Introductory Note

'Ipersonetto' ('Hypersonnet') appears in Andrea Zanzotto's
1978 collection, *Il Galateo in Bosco*, the title of which indicates
the focal points of the book. The *Galateo* is the dialogue on
good manners written by Giovanni della Casa in the 16th
century: the *Bosco* is the wood which used to cover the hills near
Zanzotto's home-village, Pieve di Soligo, not far from Treviso
in North-East Italy. It was in this woodland retreat that della
Casa composed his dialogue (and some of his poems too). But
the wood was also the scene of fierce fighting between the
Italians and the Austrians in the First World War and much of
it was destroyed. Zanzotto's poems repeatedly return, with
varying degrees of obliqueness, to these matters and to their
implications – how nature (the wood) and rules for behaviour
(the *Galateo*) come together, how what seems to have been a
symbiosis has been destroyed by violence, how poetry (which
has its conventions and yet is free) may or may not continue,
may or may not recover the past. 'Ipersonetto' brings together
much of what is scattered through the collection as a whole,

but it looks particularly to the question of conventions in poetry, especially Petrarchist ones. Zanzotto's own note says: 'The hypersonnet consists of fourteen sonnets, each of which occupies the place of a single verse in a normal sonnet, plus a preface and a conclusion. The composition is a homage to those who, like Gaspara Stampa (the16th-century Paduan poet) and Cardinal Della Casa, the author of the *Galateo*, wrote sonnets during their sojourn in the Wood.'

The originals play with the Italian Petrarchan tradition. The metre and rhyme-schemes are immediately recognisable, but not quite regular or familiar, as if they are being undermined at the same moment as they are being affectionately recreated. Similarly there are strong echoes of the idiom of 16th-century Petrarchism, but dissonance, nonsense and sudden changes of register constantly ironise and distort any nostalgic impulse. I felt that respectful translationese would convey very little of the switchback ambiguities of what Zanzotto was doing. I have aimed at rendering a sense (if not the sense) of the poems and have also tried to recreate some of their main formal and stylistic properties. I have kept a mix of idioms and the not quite regular Petrarchan rhyme scheme. From time to time I have also allowed myself to break through the limits of the regular iambic pentameter as a kind of echo of Zanzotto's way of almost overpacking his lines with strident sound-values. It was maybe a risky procedure, and certainly more laborious than the obvious alternatives. Whatever the outcome, it was also more fun.

Hypersonnet

PREFACE
(Sonnet of shying and subservience)

Manuals of manners, scattered speech, sweet screeds
just for you, leaves and shades, a splendid code . . .
Big with it you lie back and bask, my wood,
bulging and burgeoning as life rots and breeds . . .

Set running everywhere untrammelled leads,
tangling and untangling glomerule and node . . .
All clog of power and glory now unload,
modest albedos, pointers, bubbling seeds . . .

Spider that breeze disturbs, or filigree
hazily filmed in light and sound, no more
than these, my quill, shy back and subject be . . .

No weight be in the rays that from you start,
prescribing, pruning; into yourself withdraw
yourself, my sign, and your unstable art . . .

l.1. 'Manuals of manners'; in the original 'galatei', i.e. courtesy
manuals, derived from *Il Galateo,* the 16th-century dialogue by
Giovanni della Casa.

l 8. 'albedo' is a technical term for the proportion of the solar
light incident upon an element of the surface of a planet, which
is then reflected from it.

I

(Sonnet of snouts, spores and skeins)

O for some naughty nails and multiple
wee snouts to disinter the spores and skeins
of lifeless nerves, the vile sludge that remains
after the rite which we abhor but will:

to ply the lens of science – unbeaten still –
and see beyond it onto subtler planes:
o from some lynx-eyed lines the styles to strain
and fabricate the marvellous manual,

wherefrom, minute events which death has charred –
bunched corymbs, shades divine, secluded sward –
you'd rise again to tell us names and forms:

turned inside out the bellies, and outsplayed
the gullets in their filth, and the brigade
of teeth all shattered: look, these are the norms.

II

(Sonnet of interminable dental work)

Defeated teeth, with bite now almost spent,
through subtle waste iniquitously ejected,
or knocked out, wrenched, then falsely reconnected,
ah, mastications, bulimias that torment,

my dental debits endlessly augment,
in drunken ires of days and years effected:
impressions, bridges, teeth cut, crowned, corrected,
of oral trauma essence and accident.

What head I was not, neither fang nor craw
of beast or snake, no, just a dubious chain
of signs or bites a denture had impressed:

the man who foully butchers I abhor,
but more one bent on champing against vain
fate with chattering teeth in plaster dressed.

III

(Sonnet of slaughters and fancy manners)

So soothingly, you movements and you modes,
so infinitely lightsome and/or Sadic,
swings to and fro, fibres and fevers, sprayed
too thin or thick for mind or faith to know,

stasis of nought or nearly, doings slow
or speedier than wherever rays are rayed,
by pass and ford, by defile and blockade,
a net already clasps you in its silvery nodes:

a code by which tempestuous wind and rain,
heaven's limit, cauldron or cataclysm,
will, under other rules, find fury cease.

But what nice definitions, in what vein,
what fancified manners and what sophism
will find ways round these slaughters of yours, please ?

IV

(Sonnet of decline and nourishment)

Ah subtle pain, ah spikes of pines and briars,
ah shattered stems, ah leaves of vigour bled
before our gaze, ah pangs distributed
through the whole wood where autumn now expires . . .

Ah languor that to beds of straw retires:
achoo: and still the hankering to be fed,
achoo: and still all to the trough is led
by want that appetites inspires and sires.

So alimentary chains go for their mush,
and myriad mandibles rear up, are nourished,
or starved, spurred by the spittle of desire.

The rage and the concern melt in a slush
of gold, a bloodless shambles, or a pyre
lit by no flame. Pious law: for you I'll perish.

Note:

6-7: 'Achoo . . . Achoo . . .' : Zanzotto cites Tasso's *Gerusalemme Liberata*, XIII, 10 ('Che sí ? . . . Che sí ? . . .' 'How so ? . . . How so? . . .'), but says that the openings of the two lines are autumn sneezes too.

14 'Pious law' and 'I'll perish' are in Latin in the original.

V

(Sonnet of the lover and the parasite)

As swift from grass I snatch my hand away,
from grass / snake hid in briars of perfidy,
as from my crown of evening light break free,
and enterprises of the night essay,

O memory you take the road with me,
tuning the fragments, mending disarray:
once here for her my wits went all astray,
and here I sucked her sweetest succulency.

With grudging, fractious, acrid steps, I break
out yonder where the ferns and folds protrude
above the pit: I stomp past thorn and snake.

In the high yonder and soft under-regions
I boot, I loot, I slash my amorous lesions,
prove symbiosis false; it's time for food.

VI

(Night sonnet with headlights and voyeur)

Oft where in woodland deep I would submerge,
or else in pauses which the green growths maul
in mad assaults, where in louche loss converge
whatever benefits to me befall,

there where what was mine once, I know it all,
– the pungent clouds of pollen, herbs that purge
or poison, the pure honey and the gall,
the quick hours under drought's or downpour's scourge,

there where I came upon strawberries hid
by ferns or palms, or found, uplifted, wet,
the young fig gently glistening in its bower,

the voyeur, headlights on, breaks in, amid
beech, ash and oak, between the leaf and flower.
Irked, he reverses out. That makes it better.

VII

(Sonnet of woodland soma and acupuncture)

Clawmark of subtle tiger, ideogram
to which my parlous substance I commend,
in webs of yin and yang a-tremble penned,
seeking the points where living flames unjam,

whilst I am probed by needles dram by dram, –
thorns, razors, nails jabbed by a loving friend –
meridian lines through all my frame extend
as yin and yang force every diaphragm.

So do I feel, feel my dull matter so
under that hand, that tiger so extreme,
as if a thousand Cupids etched my heart.

And yet it's not that I can overthrow
your quirk, your quibble or your enthymeme.
I rave now worse than ever from your dart.

Note:

l. 13: 'enthymeme': 'in the sense of a syllogism the first part of
which remains doubtful, hidden (repressed)' (Z.)

– 'The ideogram following the poem is the one for acupuncture' (Z.)

VIII

(Sonnet of woodland brakes and bounds)

O noble wiggle, who through grassland snake,
difficult flicker which some enigma steers,
which no enigma steers, which yet puts fears
into the heart which sees snake come from brake:

nausea, from weak repose my self you take
into the void which all grass here veneers,
wherefrom lightbeam or thicket disappears
in paths, snakepaths, in sibilants of snake:

and you, my mind, oh to abide, at bounds
of grooves and joints and risks in sly dismay,
oh you who are honed where risks and bounds abound:

there is no holding me from the mêlée,
nerves, ears and eyes at once off with a bound,
if hiss of snake from fell shades comes their way.

IX

(Sonnet of Linnaeus and Dioscorides)

Light waxes and light wanes; from dewy leas
it turns and steps, true to itself, aside.
You fronds and grass swirl in a swollen tide
who for me decked the hill and dale to please.

Oh to be Linnaeus or Dioscorides,
your doings are so rich, so varified
your forms and ways, with names apter applied
than is to tongue the tang of clitoris.

But it is head, a pointed head, a-lack,
this is a snake's head, serpent's scale and back,
in which I ink you in flux, knot, or scrawl.

But mine's a non-head, neither text nor note,
not aught that springs from pen or floats from throat,
no wholesome me, not not, no whole at all.

Note:

Linnaeus is the 18th-century Swedish botanist, Dioscorides the
2nd-century Greek herbalist.

X

(Sonnet of lurking and cross-winds)

I stood and watched a chilling wind of May
undulate yesterday from field to field,
blenching the greenery, as change revealed
how trusted semblance turns to disarray.

And yet a bitter brightness strained to ray
out from dense growths that secret nests concealed,
where little close things crept and cracked and squealed,
came blindly spurting, blindly sped away,

and things ungraspable, like throngs of asps
thrust forwards in the cross-winds, like the toxic
inventions nudging us to nothingness.

Thus would I could be free from my own grasp,
from all and everyone, as the be-all is,
lurking in obscure echoes, tracks and rocks.

XI

(Sonnet of what to do and think)

What do you do ? Or think ? To whom speaks who ?
Who and what cock-a-doodle do I plumb,
with drips of what rills feed the vacuum
round me of rustic living mouldered through ?

To whom pass, for what needle to renew
that threadbare wit that leaves my poor self numb,
and why, for whom, tongue I this dum-di-dum,
talk, eloquence and music all askew ?

What do you think, who never ever were,
even in errant ghost of dream or sign,
what are you doing, dream-sign, er of er ?

Warblings of birds, of brooks, of brakes, the fraught
nothings stirring a nothing to design,
thought of non-thinking, think: what thinks your thought ?

XII

(Sonnet of semblances and form divine)

Oh show to us, your lovely semblance show –
but you have no more semblance than the spring
of light that gives the wood its watering
and nourishing, and in itself pules low.

I combed the firs in vain desire to know
of your dry transfers into the gathering
of shades that sometimes to each other cling,
or now, cold lover, from each other flow . . .

Form chaste, divine, you ulceral stigma, go
forth in your errant valour and enmesh
together stamens stelae styles afresh,

and squash them quick, where sentiment and sense
and non-sense have a different pertinence,
pure tongue-tied liquor, never-never show . . .

Note:

ll.1 and 9: 'lovely semblance' and 'form chaste, divine' are,
in the original, ('bel sembiante' and 'casta, diva') echoes of
Bellini's *Norma*

XIII

(Sonnet of Ugo, Martin and Pollicino 1778–1978)

'What salvage is a headstone for lost days?'
but what stone in these jumbled wastenesses,
what flake from cumuli and congeries
shall I pick out, alas, along the braes ?

For though I went round all the woodland ways –
pale Holzwege in serial images –,
what stone to glorify my miseries
should I diminish or what block deface ?

With crags that crumble in the bogey dark,
the world made into crags in dens of pitch,
what cemeterial manuals of life,

as low as earth, low as dead shades, will mark
at least the trace in which the hurt and strife
of lost days (night-blue pebbles!) lives: yes, which ?

Note:

Ugo is Ugo Foscolo (b.1778), the poet of *Dei sepolcri (On tombs)*,
l.10 of which is made into the opening of this sonnet: Martin
is Martin Heidegger, whose *Holzwege* ('woodland paths') appear
in l.7: Pollicino ('little chicken') is an ironic figure of the poet.

XIV

(Sonnet of vetoes and irises)

What torpid knots of root I labour under,
resistant roots that dully throb and clash,
a ceaseless labour to track down and stash
its dead sense though it stalls or falls asunder,

its living sense which glows in its own wonder
and fades where shades and groves eternal flash:
but with what roots through miles of earth I gnash,
and in what grisly growths twist back and blunder.

I give green sheen to plumbeous earth and root,
and rampant vetoes I dig out and dump,
and then I faint, and in my asthma slump.

I'm blood run dry, though in odd spots I leak:
I am an old snuffling mole, yet ruin wreak:
in lead I spy iris on iris shoot.

POSTSCRIPT

(Infamy sonnet and mandala)
To F. Fortini

You sum of unreal summits, my land, you
flake into nought, yet visibly sustain
grubs changing into gods, turn loss to gain,
and make invention and emprise anew.

Your strivings trip from untrue to untrue,
but in such various and unending chain
that all that here is rottenness or bane
there to a match or meld with truth slips through.

And I, false too, clone of so false a breed,
or addled, with the father's fault made worse,
make packing words my deed or my misdeed.

Thus have I used you once more to my end,
sonnet, you infamous, purloining verse,
mandala in which my beggar's crusts are penned.

Tom Cheesman
Owain Glyndŵr Explained to an Algerian Asylum Seeker – Act V

The poetry of Soleïman Adel Guémar was sampled in *MPT* 3/2 (2004). He came to Swansea (where I live) in 2002 at the behest of the Home Office's National Asylum Support Service, having fled political violence in Algeria. Late one evening in spring 2004, when he had still not yet been granted refugee status, we were driving into Swansea down the high side of the Tawe valley, above the suburb of Landore. He remarked that the view toward the bay – especially at night – strongly reminded him of Algiers, and that this provided some consolation in his exile.

Another kind of after-image crossed with this to spur these part-parodic verses. I read in the Welsh magazine *Planet* of the Harri Webb Memorial Prize 2004, calling for poems on Owain Glyndŵr. The uprising of 1400–1409 saw him crowned Owain IV of Wales, but after it was put down, and the English retook their main fortress at Harlech, Glyndŵr vanished from history into legend: he was never captured, and no one knows when or where he died. It occurred to me to invent a last act of his tragedy, set in Algiers. Being an English incomer, fairly innocent of Welsh history and lore, I mugged up on Glyndŵr from various sources, but relied mainly on fancy. Welsh elegies and English mockeries alike (Shakespeare's 'Glendower') are rich in astronomical prognostications: hence my 'more meteors'. George Borrow's *Wild Wales* gave me the term Lloegrians (meaning the English). The blank verse aims to be redolent of Welsh traditional poetry – densely alliterative and assonant – and I used mock-francophone alexandrines (italicised) for lines directly addressed to the real subject, Guémar.

He provided me with the names for Glyndŵr in exile, in the languages of oppressor and oppressed. Qumri (Cymru, Wales) means 'dove' in Arabic. Awen Ath-Qlad-Yur phonetically approximates Owain Glyndŵr in Tamazight, the Berber language of Kabylia, which has been formally accorded cultural rights in Algeria since 2002. Guémar assures me that it is a plausible proper name. I learned only after submitting the poem that 'awen', aptly enough, is Welsh for 'muse'.

Other, much less crucial after-images: the title alludes to Tahar Ben Jalloun's *Le Racisme expliqué à ma fille*; the double (past and present) narrative dimly echoes Orhan Pamuk's *The White Castle*; and of three lines I have now revised for *MPT*, one shows the influence of Christopher Logue's stupendous *War Music*.

Guémar's collection, *State of Emergency* (a parallel text edition, with translations by me and John Goodby) is due to appear in Arc Publications' 'Visible Poets' series in 2007.

The end of his story is poorly attested:
in Welsh or in English the sources are suspect.
His features are strange but his fate is familiar . . .

Steering well clear of Harlech, sore and raw,
skirting Sycharth, heart aching for Margaret,
hunted, night-walking, unwitnessed he crossed
part of the land of the Lloegrians, till
he made the Cornish coast. He crept to wake
one of Northumberland's men, a wrecker.
More meteors saw them unmoor a small craft
and row slowly straight into the low waves.
They headed west and out of sight of land –
Barbary slavers intercepted them.

The cosmopolitan crew knew bugger all
about Cymru – but a man of power,
his retainer cursing his unlucky
loyalty to a fugitive, they knew.
Unconvinced that any Irish prince would pay
the rich rewards Owain vainly promised,
they slit the wrecker's throat and shipped the master's
curiosity value chained in the hold
back through Biscay, past the Rock and onward
to the Roman-Berber city of Algiers.

Your city's ugly loveliness is not unlike
the one we write in now, or so you told me once:
the valleys, hills and bay, the petrochemicals,
the prison by the beach, the struggling terraces,
seen under sodium skies from above Landore
in exile's black uncanny insomniac eye,
recall the setting of all your writing – the way
your presence here involuntarily evokes
his ghostly otherness six centuries ago.

As Owain waits to be bought at auction
his sad account arouses scant interest:
the northern islands lack political
or intellectual significance,
their coastal waters corsairs' plunder-hoards:
coins, gems, rude metalwork, plum shes and hes
and sundry semi-savage exotica.

No valuables or documents backed up
the noble slave's outlandish narrative.
Spain's representatives unwillingly
sent to the court to check his royal claim,
but storms or pirates took the messenger.
His owner put Owain to work, draining
swamps, building villas, harbour walls, quarrying.

Slowly he learned the local linguas francas,
the rulers' Arabic, the workers' Tamazight,
enough to start to cast his story as a song,
as if he'd leisure, which in his head he had:
art engrossed Owain. He universalised
in verse the tale he couldn't help but tell –
not fearing it unsung, save this final fifth:
the elegies would keep his name alive –
he, however, had to be his own teller.

Seven long years he'd been in chains when
laughing pashas heard him sing the tragedy
of Wan Ben el-Qumri's revolt and downfall
in barbaric but richly timbred Arabic.
In Tamazight, in contrast, his performance passed
from tongue to tongue to become the deathless
ballad that is still a pillar of Kabyle
traditional cultural identity:
'Awen Ath-Qlad-Yur'.

And when they came for him,
this immigrant voice of national consciousness,
the manacles they hammered from his limbs
were Welsh-made, and he yelled he'd claimed asylum,
but the priests and monks were out of earshot.
Fairly confident of immortality
in two corners of this world at least, Owain
now turns his fork-bearded face away from us.

Translations from the eye
Two poems by Robert Hull

There's something tantalising about old white-black negatives. Not the copper-brown miniatures of these days – speaking pre-digitally – but eloquent artefacts the size, often enough, of the black-and-white photographs they translate or reverse into. The excitement that goes with stumbling unexpectedly on a cache of old pictures is one thing. The drawn-out anticipation attendant on the conversion of negatives into glimpses of what was, which goes with sending them off to the print-shop and waiting and collecting and finally seeing, is another entirely. Moreover, while the photograph you come upon by chance is already unavoidable, the negative offers the option of speculation, and of refusal, or deferral. One print of my mother on the deck of a ship somewhere, another of her dressed somewhat in the manner of Suzanne Lenglen, the Wimbledon women's tennis champion of 1919, were the last I had done into light-of-day actuality.

The painting referred to is one of a handful that have prompted writing, writing that has been less though about the paintings per se than about aspects of context – one's own guilt here, her over-editing of a spontaneous talent in another piece, and so on. Oddly perhaps, her one complete and strikingly

achieved artistic talent – as a very fine pianist – hasn't educed
the same kind of homage. There's a title – *My mother met
Rachmaninov* – but no poem yet.

Black and White

A thick wad of negatives
in an old Williams Deacon's
Bank envelope, an archaeology
of extinct registration numbers,
white hedges and fences,
shadowy seaside hotels.

From the print shop I recover
a group of fey children
in Sunday best with hats,
a still-life motorbike
with its arc of number-plate
over the front wheel,
horses pulling a carnival float
drowning in flowers.

I eventually find you –
a you I've never seen,
would hardly have guessed at,
dramatically Lenglen-esque
at a tennis party, stylish
in a fine scarf thrown
flamboyant round your shoulders

on the deck of a boat steaming
I can't imagine where
through the faded century's
twenties and your own.

That will do for now.
I don't want to lure
from obscurity any more
of those long-faded moments,
imagine any more clearly
these heady expeditions
in open-top motors
out on the moors somewhere,
you and three smiling friends
bowling down long white lanes
of incandescent shadow
under some far summer's
thunderous dark.

Anniversary

I didn't reckon your pictures all that much

Their clouds were too like clouds
their blues too blue

So I didn't say much
except I liked them

This one
has been in my room since you died
ten years of its waves
whitely breaking on rocks
of its clouds
drifting silently towards me

All that time
the bay the harbour wall
the gentle boats at anchor
have been getting more real
more watchable

Until now I see
a picture that says not all that much
and obviously
but says it so well
that it becomes you

Now I wish I'd said more
about that harbour where people
still go about their still lives
about these quiet nervous waves
that don't quite rhyme
I wish I'd said it
while there was time.

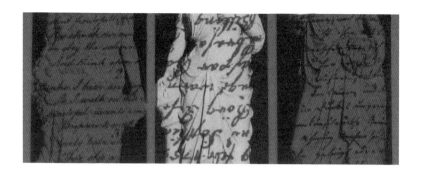

R. Cheran
'I could forget all this . . .'
Translated by Lakshmi Holmström

R. Cheran was born in Alaveddy in Jaffna, Sri Lanka, and
began writing poetry at an early age. His two early collections
Irandaavathu suriya uthayam (The second sunrise) (1982) and
Yaman (God of Death) (1984), together with an anthology of
Tamil resistance poems, *Maranatthul vaalvom* (Amidst death,
we live) which he edited in 1985, are all landmarks in
contemporary Tamil poetry. His most recent work is a
collection of poems, *Miindum kadalukku* (Once more, the
sea), published in 2004. In 1999 Cheran received a creative
non-fiction award from the Banff Centre for the Arts, Alberta,
Canada. He is currently a professor in the Department of
Sociology and Anthropology at the University of Windsor,
Canada.

I could forget all this

I could forget all this
Forget the flight
headlong through Galle Road
clutching an instant's spark of hope
refusing to abandon this wretched
vulnerable life
even though all directions shuddered
– and with them, my heart –

Forget the sight
of a thigh-bone protruding
from an upturned, burnt-out car

a single eye fixed in its staring
somewhere between earth and sky

empty of its eye
a socket, caked in blood

on Dickman's Road, six men dead
heads split open
black hair turned red

a fragment of a sari
that escaped burning

bereft of its partner
a lone left hand
the wrist wrenched off

a Sinhala woman, pregnant,
bearing, unbearably,
a cradle from a burning house

I could forget all this
forget it all, forget everything

But you, my girl,
snatched away and burnt
one late afternoon
as you waited in secret
while the handful of rice
– found after so many days –
cooked in its pot,
your children hidden beneath the tea bushes
low-lying clouds shielding them above –
How shall I forget the broken shards
and the scattered rice
lying parched upon the earth?

Waldo Williams
'The Dead Children'
Translated by Damian Walford Davies

Waldo Williams (1904–71) is arguably the greatest Welsh-language poet of the twentieth century on the strength of his only collection, *Dail Pren (Leaves of a Tree,* 1956). Quaker, pacifist, anti-imperialist and (in Anthony Conran's words) 'patron saint of the language movement', he remains a cultural icon in Wales.

The Dead Children

See these bodies of children.
They died as night
fell. They got stones
in sling volleys and shelter
then. The sun's heat failed;
she, their mainsun,

failed, with her kiss
and coddle, because
of the world's stones,
because of its snake.

See how each side is
many cuts. See the thin
thighs, how huge the
knees. They didn't get
the failure of their
'Sandwich, mum'. Their pallid
faces stung; her songs
charmed only the snake-
bite out of the dark.
They died let down.

See these bodies of children.
White and black and
yellow. Scores. The brute
snakes quiet over
borders; where his cold
torque strikes, the air
quivers. Say who gave
it sway over the green
earth? – a mad con-
junction of stars: 'You
must! You must!' Damn
you who fire the star
that damns the earth.

Mario Luzi
Two Poems
Translated by Elizabeth MacDonald

'Mario Luzi was a witness for our time.' – Carlo Azeglio Ciampi, President of Italy.

Mario Luzi's career as a poet spanned seven decades and twice earned him a nomination for the Nobel Prize for literature. His first collection (*La barca*) appeared in 1935 when he was twenty-one years of age. Despite his youth, his talent was immediately recognised, and in particular his 'exemplary imagination' (Carlo Bo). With this collection he established himself as a member of the Hermetic Movement, founded in the 1920s by Giuseppe Ungaretti and Eugenio Montale. By 1940 Luzi had become its leading exponent with collections such as *Avvento notturno* (1940), *Un brindisi* (1946) and *Quaderno gotico* (1947). His poetry at this time is characterized by an affinity with Symbolism, resulting in allusive lyrics of great beauty and remarkable technical mastery.

Nevertheless, even at this early stage, certain enduring themes are evident. Luzi was a young man during World War II, and this gave rise to his preoccupation with the effects of war and violence, and the absence of liberty. His poetry can be seen as a tireless exploration of the negative effects of history. Another recurring motif also present is Luzi's certainty of the spiritual nature of the universe. For him, this offered a means for intuitive understanding complementary to the lessons of history.

From the 1950s onwards then, the Hermetic phase was not abandoned, but rather amplified and enlarged upon, producing collections such as *Primizie del deserto* (1952), *Onore del vero* (1957), *Il giusto della vita* (1960). Then in 1963 came a turning point. With the collection *Nel magma* came a need to delve into contingency, giving rise to a style less reliant on aesthetic perfection and more prose-orientated. This afforded Luzi scope for grappling with juxtaposed themes such as time and eternity, change and identity, being and becoming. Such is the sway that time holds over our lives, he remarked, that man can conceive of eternity only as an infinite quantity of time.

To this period belong other collections such as *Dal fondo delle campagne* (1965), *Su fondamenti invisibili* (1971), *Al fuoco della controversia* (1978), *Per il battesimo dei nostri frammenti* (1985), *Frasi e incisi di un canto salutare* (1990).

The last great period opens with *Viaggio terrestre e celeste di Simone Martini* (1994), and concludes with *Dottrina dell' estremo principiante* (2004). This late flowering has produced poetry of a crystalline beauty, permeated by an exploration of the transcendental. Never a mere magnifying glass, Luzi's poetry here acquires the qualities of a prism, in which the play of light and colour throw into relief a mind questing for meaning and truth.

As a playwright, Luzi achieved eminence. His most recent works include *Felicità turbate* (Garzanti, 1995) and *Ceneri e ardori* (Garzanti, 1997). He was also a renowned translator, especially of French literature.

Mario Luzi belongs to an artistic elect, representing, perhaps, a new frontier of alternativism. He is one of the very few great artists in whom the polarizing divisions of Yeats's dictum, that there can be perfection of either the life or the work, have been healed. His lasting testimony is to show how, instead, life and work can feed seamlessly and creatively into each other.

Mario Luzi died peacefully in his sleep on Monday 28th February 2005.

Night falls

Night falls with the long
drawn out song of the owl,
scattering lights around the coomb,
inching shakily up its humid slopes.
The strength gained over long
years of suffering fails me
and half-baked theories are disarmed,
this manly smile
has lost its composure.

Just who are you
lying in wait like an invisible sentinel
at that turning point in age
until your moment had come? To you
I owe this time of gratitude
replete with grief.

And now foreboding worms its way in,
seeping into these early summer nights,
overrunning the wall still warm to the touch,
pursuing the fireflies hovering in farmyards,
fanning out into the lanes where suddenly,
in a glare of headlights, a hare darts by.

My dear, how could I have failed to see it?
Life itself was in abeyance
as it is now in this vigil.
I could weep for thinking
how I marred this long wait
with so many inadequate words,
so many rash irredeemable gestures,
and now, scarred, nothing else matters to me
but that this torment come to an end.

'Salvation sought after like this does not behove
either you or those like you. Peace,
if it comes, will come to you by other ways
more lucid, more hard-won than this,
when to suffer no longer seems futile;
for affliction also exists and must live and
transmute into your good and that of others.
Faith dwells within you, faith is a person.'

This song has sung itself out.

All Hallows (1954)

Fire everywhere, the fire of slow-burning stubble, fire
flickering against the walls, its shadow
too faint to etch itself there, fire
farther out again steepling up and down
the hill for its haul of ash,
fire flaking down from the branches and pergolas.

Neither beforehand nor afterwards but properly
in the here and now where all around me, joyous
and sad, the valley is drained of life, drained of
fire, I pause to take stock of my dead ones
and the roll-call seems to lengthen, unfurling
from leaf to leaf down as far as the first stump.

Grant them rest, eternal rest, a
safe passage far from this flurry of
ash and flame that clogs up and
chokes our throats, then scatters along
the lanes, falters in flight, and vanishes;
let death be death, truly
death: strifeless, lifeless.
Grant them rest, eternal rest, appease them.

Down there where the decimation runs deeper
people are ploughing, drawing pails of water,
muttering their way through the stillness of change
hour by hour. A puppy stretches out over
in the corner of the orchard, and dozes off.

Such a slow-burning fire is barely enough,
if even that, to light up for a while
this life in the shadowlands. Another,
only another might do the rest and
whatever else it takes: consume those remains,
transform them into incorruptible bright light.

Prayers from the dead for the living, prayers
of the living and the dead in a flame. Kindle it,
for the night is upon us, the night encroaches,
enmeshing the mountains in its spider-like quiver;
soon our eyes will be of no use, all that remains is
knowledge emblazoned or darkness.

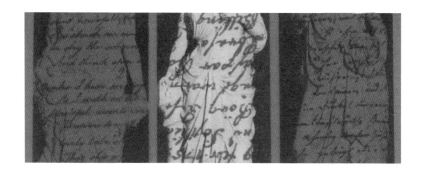

Dorothea Grünzweig
Three Poems
Translated by Derk Wynand

Dorothea Grünzweig, born in Korntal, Germany in 1952, studied German and English at the Universities of Tübingen and Bangor. After a period of research on G.M. Hopkins at Oxford and a teaching position at the Scottish University of Dundee, she worked at a boarding school in southern Germany. Except for brief terms as writer-in-residence in Scotland and Germany, since 1989 she has lived in Helsinki, Finland, where she writes and translates works by Finnish and English-language poets. She has published three collections of poems, *Mittsommerschnitt* (1997), for which she received the Lyrikpreis der Stiftung Niedersachsen/ Wolfenbüttel, *Vom Eisgebreit (From the Ice Field)* 2000, and *Glasstimmen lasinäänet (Glass Voice lasinäänet)* 2004, for which she received the Christian-Wagner Prize for Poetry – all with Wallstein Verlag, Göttingen. Derk Wynand has translated a good deal of her poetry.

Glorification by Snow

And even in winter the house
has no window that admits a split
between inside and out

in its light the winter bed has
taught us to lie down because
the crowns of birches and pines
lying like this can be seen
uncut and snow
as it seeps from the sky

The moon sweeps over the icefield
its howls of joy echoing
like the bright storm's in our ears
dilating into hollows
where alternately we can lie
knee against chest all to ourselves and
one in the other listening
snowglorified

not like the woodpheasant snowmute
clawing a slender branch
foxfear flashing through its sleep
can lie fearfree each in the other

till the snow one day in distant March
must let its life go

Since winter's eartime
                    our house
on the hill hearkens far out
into the land where shrill piercing
sounds flail down to earth

In the riot of sound
as if some quiet
sweetpleading thing
were issuing now from shafts
and then from towers
                    It must be that church's pealing
one day on our departure dashed
and now resounding in its struggle
to rise again from the depths

Struck to an image by the bells
father at the altar
in the shadow of wings spread
out over the children us
holding heavy black hymnals
offering ourselves smiling
                    our thin voices strings
to the same pitch sisterly strung
serving the Lamb

Winter because we want
to grasp it it's the pealing
                    is it not of that fatherchurch
turns into waiting
bound to the window's crosspiece
a fleeting finding

How fine our children seemed
hearing the fleshly names of things
though we didn't know how
to go about it until
guests came calling a cat a child
        and around us a garden grew

Now we're drifting childward again
that nature leading to what's brighter lighter
to a shift in our nature
        an opening of ears
we need fewer external ties
only the mail silently crossing the silence

        Now fleshly names can be found
They're not just said as repeats of things
or pinned to them and the softest tap
will break them loose
        true names lie at the core of things
        indeed came before those things
that grew around them
names that lead away from the hitandmiss
in our lives and our thingsuffering
they cheer us on beyond the fleshly names
        Can you not see that we live
        you should also live

We lie on autumn's edge with relaxed
external ties only by way of mail silently crossing the silence
the cats purring on our laps the child playing around us

Maples and birches have been set aflame
we are awake as bells we dream
and a warmth that shakes us up
        flows out of things

Vyacheslav Kupriyanov
Four poems
Translated by Dasha C. Nisula

It is not unusual for Russian writers to be sought by publishers abroad. In fact, this has been the case with many Russian writers of fiction and poetry especially in the twentieth century. So it is not surprising that Vyacheslav Kupriyanov's work, especially his free verse, has appeared in print in many European languages. His work has been published in Poland, Bulgaria, Croatia, Macedonia and Yugoslavia, Germany and England, and Sri Lanka.

Vyacheslav Kupriyanov was born in Novosibirsk, Russia, in 1939. He completed his studies in 1967 at the Institute of Foreign Languages in Moscow, in the department of mechanical translation and mathematical linguistics. He translated Austrian and German poets, Rilke, Hölderlin, and Novalis among others, as well as American poets. It took some time, however, for Vyacheslav Kupriyanov to see his own first collection of poetry in print. When it finally appeared in 1981, *Ot pervovo litsa (First Person)*, Kupriyanov was already forty-two years old. His second collection, *Zhizn' idet (Life Goes On)*, came out the very next year, in 1982, and two more collections followed, *Domashnie zadaniya (Homework)* in 1986 and *Echo* in

1988. Another collection, *Stikhi* (*Poems*), appeared in print in 1994. Poems for this translation were taken from selected poetry *Lychshie vremena* (*Better Times*), published in Moscow in 2003.

Along with Vladimir Burich, Vyacheslav Kupriyanov is one of the few poets in Russia cultivating expression in free verse. Though free verse has threads in old Slavic poetic tradition, Kupriyanov's work in also reminiscent of the translation work he has done himself from English, namely poetry by Walt Whitman and Carl Sandburg. It is in simple expressions that we find his profound message on the human condition at the end of the twentieth century. Kupriyanov is a master of the Russian language. After all, he is a child of the mid-twentieth century who understands the logos. He plays with a word, with the Russian word-root, with prefixes and suffixes, he creates neologisms, forcing the translator to the wall, exclaiming – it cannot be done in a non-Slavic language! And yet, what Kupriyanov has to say is just as important as how he says it. The *what* is certainly not what is lost in translation. The poet's love for the individual, nature, and the universe surfaces in any language. He worries that our contemporary man not only has transformed and alienated himself, but the whole universe.

Vyacheslav Kupriyanov is a poet, prose writer, translator, and critic who is constantly in search of the truth. He loves to awaken his readers with unexpected forms and in the process draws on the long tradition of Russian experimental writers. From the early-twentieth-century poetry by Mayakovsky to the end-of-the-twentieth-century work by Kupriyanov, the play with words in the Russian literary language remains strong and vibrant.

Contemporary Man – 2

Contemporary man
extends himself through the wire
together with the murmur of the sea
jams himself into the shell of the telephone
compresses himself
seeks immortality
on a phonograph record
becomes a sea monster
a prisoner of the television aquarium
he becomes more portable
more compact
more contemporary
already he can be switched on
switched off
made louder softer
he doesn't see you
doesn't hear you
he doesn't know you

History of Mail

For 300 years
Russians claimed
oppression by the Mongols
who it turns out
were just delivering the mail
for 300 years
Russia received letters
it couldn't read
that's why Moscow
had to be burned intermittently
in order to free itself from the darkness
of unread letters

finally Ivan the Terrible
went East
took Kazan and began
to send letters West
to the runaway Prince Kurbskoy
these terrible letters
were answered by Peter the Great
from abroad from Holland

then Catherine also the Great
arranged a connection with the better world
of Mr Voltaire then Napoleon
the very Bonaparte who by the continuous burning
of Moscow helped introduce
the elegant French epistolary style
for nobility so as not to confuse
the common folk
too soon with
freedom equality and fraternity

with better delivery of mail
Decembrists sent their letters
about reforming Russia
from Siberia to awaken
Herzen in London
they were answered by
Vladimir Ilych squinting
his farsighted Mongolian gaze
from Geneva from Zurich

then the October Revolution
came to pass
as an inevitable consequence
of Mongolian mail
as an Eastern
reply and a challenge to the West

in the next 300 years
something will come to us as a response
from the West
by electronic mail

Landscape with Polyphemus

All this is reflected:

Sisyphus is pushing his rock
Icarus is falling into the sea
Prometheus is chained to a cliff

while carelessly rollick
indifferent nymphs
apolitical fauns
in the ecstasy
of a fleeting life

all this is reflected
in the blood-shot
single eye of Polyphemus

that is just about to be gouged
by a wanderer
seeking his homeland
Odysseus

Optimistic Geography

North America
still hasn't slipped
into South America

Asia Major
still hasn't crushed
Central and Asia Minor

Europe still hasn't fallen
through the Mediterranean
onto free Africa

Africa still
hasn't been swallowed
by the Sahara

Icebergs of Antarctica
still haven't succeeded in
merging with the ice
of Greenland

Forces of gravity
still surpass
any
armed forces

The political map of the world
hasn't been destroyed
by the physical map

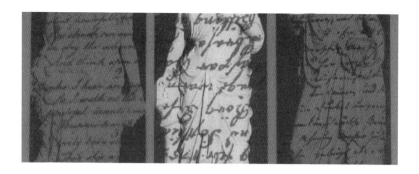

Naomi Jaffa
Poets and their Translators at the Aldeburgh Festival

This year's eighteenth Aldeburgh Poetry Festival will feature two outstanding Europeans. Joan Margarit began writing in Spanish but switched languages in 1978 to return to his mother tongue and is now recognised as a major Catalan voice. He is compellingly translated by Scottish poet Anna Crowe and the first UK publication of a generous selection from his eight collections – *Tugs in the Fog* (Bloodaxe) – will be launched at Aldeburgh. The programme also presents Durs Grünbein, born in 1962 and widely acknowledged to be Germany's leading poet of his generation. Michael Hofmann's versions of his selected poems *Ashes for Breakfast* (Faber) provides a brilliant introduction to his work for UK readers. It must be significant that, after translating more than forty books from German, Grünbein is the first contemporary poet that Hofmann has chosen to work with.

Aldeburgh has always been committed to showcasing international poetry, bringing a wide variety of the best poets in the world to a small seaside town in Suffolk. In only its second year the Festival programmed Miroslav Holub and Marin Sorescu, and to date, poets from at least thirty-four countries have been represented. This doesn't just benefit us as individuals, it's crucial for English poetry too, to be informed by different traditions.

In the last three years we've been privileged to experience at first hand Mourid Barghouti (Palestine), Fadhil Al-Azzawi (Iraq) and Aharon Shabtai (Israel). No flannel. Just the vital immediacy of poems and the insights and empathy they can generate. To hear the poems read by the poet is always mind-expanding and revives our aural pleasure in language. This is true even – and maybe especially – if one doesn't understand the language. The obviously eloquent, but to us meaningless, words are a welcome challenge to the reliability of our everyday assumptions and belief systems.

Of course only really good poets make really good translators. As Michael Hofmann writes: 'You have to look comfortable, voluntary. The Grünbein translations will look like – I hope to God they do look like – not the product of steel rulers and midnight oil, but like poems that want to be poems.' And for this reason we always honour translators equally at Aldeburgh, inviting them to read their English versions and offering both poets the same flat-rate fee. We also like to celebrate the partnership and the often wonderfully warm on-stage interaction.

The new UK collections by Durs Grünbein and Joan Margarit have recently been announced as the PBS 'Recommended Translations' for Autumn and Winter 2006. And both poets will be part of the Festival's characteristically diverse line-up which will include Finuala Dowling (South Africa), Peter Fallon (Ireland), Vona Groarke (Ireland), Choman Hardi (Kurdistan), three outstanding Americans – Philip Levine, Naomi Shihab Nye and Sharon Olds – and Alastair Reid (Scotland) who was Pablo Neruda's favourite translator. Plus Vicki Feaver, Jenny Joseph, Nick Laird, Jon Stallworthy, John Powell Ward and many more – almost all reading for the first time at Aldeburgh.

18th Aldeburgh Poetry Festival, 3–5 November 2006,
full details available from www.thepoetrytrust.org
For a printed programme or further information:
info@thepoetrytrust.org or 01986 835950.

Joan Margarit
Six poems
Translated by Anna Crowe

Joan Margarit was born in 1938 during the Spanish Civil War in Sanauja, La Segarra region, in Catalonia. One of Spain's best known architects, from 1968 until retirement he was Professor of Structural Calculations at Barcelona's School of Architecture. He originally wrote in Spanish, but in 1978 he switched languages and is now recognised as a major Catalan poet. His *Tugs in the Fog* (Bloodaxe), a selection of work from eight collections, is his first English book and will be launched at the 2006 Aldeburgh Poetry Festival.

The motives of the wolf

Intimate efficient
and taciturn, the sea.
It cannot bear the affected
sentimental lament,
or melancholy,
if it is nothing but cowardice.
Far away from you, beside the water,
there's someone with a dog that's leaping
and snapping at the waves,
trying to destroy them.
How many people will a winter
beach have spoken to
of deceits and disappointments?
From the inhospitable sand
how many will their own hell
have drawn with force?
It's hard in winter. The hunger
for love in the icy woods
renders the wolf tame,
as it circles a well
gazing at the pure image
of the moon in its depths.
The wolf keeps watch over
how life runs away
from among moral pacts
made of subtle deceits.
Marriage and family
have never made poetry,
they are an alibi
of the solitary wild beast
that licks itself and conceals
feelings of blame

following with bent head
this dog's path.
Sometimes it howls
and, in silence, remembers.
Then it wants to be saved.
Fierce, old, tired,
growling, showing its teeth,
it leaps at the throat of the present.
At first it's a stray dog
that the lonely man takes in,
but it is in fact the wolf,
cruel, melancholy,
its eyes ever gleaming
from so many unresolved dreams.
This is the couple –
the person and the beast –
that you see in the distance
walking along the beach.

Return to Turó Park

Higher and darker, the laurels cover
the green bronze horses in the middle of the lake.
When the past turns into dream
beneath the trees that no longer exist,
like luxury in days gone by the park spreads
its dark green colour in the depths of your eyes:
the summer's pink rains still fall
on the eucalyptus, and the voices
that now wait for oblivion. The shady pool
has kept its water-lilies,
shades of white dresses as an evening falls
like the moon in the breast of gloomy cypresses.

Lost war

Dawn makes the city squalid,
a stucco sickness, architecture
of shopkeepers and Wagner, a history
with symbols as vulgar as defeat
and the whores of the port, and greed.
Yet, still, reflected in the asphalt there is
the loneliness of an even dirtier city
where the one you will be on your last
winter walk is decaying already. Poetry
has consoled you with the solitary's
ancient cunning, but there always comes
the moment of defeat in a struggle
where, in losing love, you lose life.

Beside the beach

He guards the cars every night
on open ground, next to the restaurant.
In the early hours, beside the bonfire
in his dreams he murders beautiful women
and, with expensive cognacs, sets fire to the wind.
Thus hatred kindles in his eyes
a flame that burns the black metals
and misted windows of the empty cars.
The guests leave, and their money
and the discreet smile which wisely
the women slip him mollify him and,
already weary, racked with sleep, he listens
to the sea hidden behind the shadows.

Television in the service of traumatology
for Carles Villanueva and Juan José Madrigal

Night draws in. With empty sofas all around,
they let the light from the screen enter
the dark cavern of their dreams.
One of them, legless – the rumble of a train
sometimes seems to cross his brow –
has placed a cigar between the lips of the other,
who left his arms to an electricity pylon.
In the dubious light of desire, when
the coldest and most sensual woman appears,
each adds himself to the other in watching her,
becoming a single man as ideal as she is.

Recalling El Besòs (1980)
for Carles Buxadé

The windows at night, with their yellow light,
are eyes outlined with the asphalt's mascara.
I remember the flat: the light-bulb dead,
dogs and babies on a mattress.
In the putrefying kitchen, with no door,
mould on the stacks of unwashed plates,
a boy is listening to an old pick-up that's playing
records from a junk-shop, but all Bach.
The black high-tension cables
shine in the moonlight above the river.
Beneath the raised-up sweep of motorway,
the desolate no man's land,
secondhand-car pound.
For this world, no other future but Bach.

Durs Grünbein
Three Poems
Translated by Michael Hofmann

Durs Grünbein was born in Dresden in the former East Germany in 1962. He has lived in Berlin since 1985, working as poet, essayist and translator from English, Latin and Greek, and now as Professor at the Kunstakademie Düsseldorf. He won Germany's major literary prize, the Georg-Büchner-Preis, at the age of 33. *Ashes for Breakfast* (Faber), his ninth book of poems and his first in English translation, will be launched at the 2006 Aldeburgh Poetry Festival.

To a Cheetah in the Moscow Zoo

Furs this expensive you normally only find wrapped around
    the shoulders
Of gangsters' molls outside the casino, movements this
    slinky
Only on the catwalk from the androgynous models,
Eyes dilating in the flashbulbs. As lean a feline
As Pisanello once painted with ravished brush
(The fur spotted, whiskery, a golden fleece).
She sashays swishing up and back. Her spine measures out
The least movement.
                            To change direction
Millimeters in front of the ditch is something for which
She doesn't even need eyes. There's nothing out there
For the ear or the sensitive nose but the noise and sweat
Beyond the wire fence, where those monkeys congregate
With their baby carriages at visiting time. Her breath
Coming hard, she magics the fetor of the metropolis
Into a charmed ozone...the white ribbons
In the girls' hair into strips of gazelle meat. Her fine head
No bigger than your fist, keeps its alert posture
As she spies zebras in the flickering at the gates of Moscow.
Then she yawns, the prisoner of the cement.

Berlin Posthumous

You can always go to Berlin. Remember, you've been there before.
                                        Kierkegaard, *Repetition*

December morning. Driving past the cemetery walls in the
    taxi,
You feel a strange pang of envy. '*Their* worries are over.'
In your eyes, forced apart by light, you have a sensation as of
    wet sand.
The driver is fingering his worry-beads. You see nothing but
    biers
In the windows, junk, behind yellow drawn curtains.
And then you begin counting. The fingers of both hands
Are not enough for all the undertakers on the stretch
Between your front door and the station, all hustling
    shamelessly
For the dead of tomorrow. A cutthroat business, evidently.
Everything here is right angles. Crosses and latticework cure
    you
Of your yen to die as a samurai with a sword in your guts.
The bakers have kneaded their dough. Different fruit gleams
    in flats.
The butchers are whetting their blades before getting to
    work.
The taximeter skips ahead twenty cents at a time – money it
    takes
Forever to earn if what you do for a living is turn
    hexameters.
A delicate shiver in your brain, the effect of so much
    cynicism
Taken on an empty stomach, first thing in the morning.
Silently you catch the eye of the driver in the rearview
    mirror.

He will have to step on it if you're not to miss your train.
6.03, a low voice gabbles financial news on the car radio.
A raiding party on some stock exchange, someone else's
    credit rating dives.
'Ever considered the future?' the bold print mugs you in
    Coffins for all the Family.
On the pavement edge, a life flashes by – a blur and gone.
'What's the sense in endless moping. Just leave us to do the
    coping.'

Arcadia for All

It's not just the city centre, deserted on Sunday morning,
The letters, branded with the stamp *not known at this address,*
The sea-surge in the phone, and the irked yell of 'Pardon?'
The thousands of cars abandoned at the roadside by their
    owners;
It's also the advertising hoardings with the poetic
    borrowings that no one reads,
The defaced monuments to boyhood heroes in the parks,
All this and much more, from which you prefer to avert your
    gaze –
Well, it gives you pause. This, then, swollen to metropolitan
    dimensions,
Is what it looks like, the place where they buried god like a
    dog.
Arcadia, celestial cemetery, a model for every city
Where death comes and goes, and life stutters on privatized
    astroturf.
Forget your idylls, your landscape of the blessed, your
    bucolic reservations.

Whatever the shepherds sang or travellers dreamed –
This here's the place for you. *City* and *gorod, metropolis* or
   ville.
Here you promenade your own soul, beneath stoical trees,
A glass man, insomniac, reflected in so much excess.
The tempo's set by glances, flashing eye-contacts, not
   eclogues
Of flirtatious Daphne, Milon and Lakon closer than a pair of
   brothers.
You can feel the buzz in your bones, your spine in the judder
   of the arcades,
Lose your face, dazzled from the metallic upgleam of the
   puddles,
But where else is home? It was only ever here, in this
   familiar exile
When you crept into your rathole at night, that you tasted a
   few crumbs of joy.
When else, if not in the human flock, maundering without
   purpose,
Did you feel so alive, so cut adrift from the mouldering
   posthumous peace?

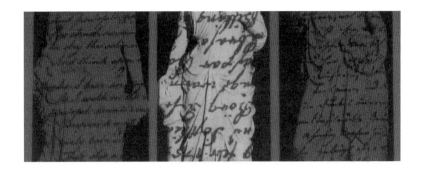

Peter France
In Memory of Gennady Aygi: Translation and Community

On February 21 this year the Russian poet Gennady Aygi died in a Moscow hospital. He had been suffering from terminal cancer for some months. Just over a month before his death, however, on an exceptionally cold January evening, he had come in from the snowy suburbs to the Chekhov Library in central Moscow to give what was to be his last reading. It was a moving occasion, the more so for me as I had to catch a plane back to Scotland the next morning, and I knew I was saying a last goodbye to a dear friend of over thirty years as we slithered over the ice to the jeep that was to take him back to his flat.

The evening began, surprisingly, with a group of my English translations – a warm-up for the real business of the evening, but also a gesture of welcome to the foreign visitor; so I read, for instance, the following poem from *Veronica's Book*, a collection of 1983 devoted to Aygi's daughter's first six months:

Beginning of the 'Period of Likenesses'

and the forces
of the tribe are stirred – and they float
and turn like wind-and-light – carrying over your face
cloud after cloud: all expressions
of vanished faces –

to manifest to confirm – the 'definitive'
appearance – your own:

with fire – standing firm in turbulence! –

(is it not with this same heat that – peering – I shudder:

as if – amid some singing? –

pain – came in like the wind)

The bond and continuity with earlier generations – with Aygi's
own Chuvash forebears – is characteristic of this poet for whom
poetry – including translation – was an act of communion
between individuals, generations and whole peoples.

It was possible to begin with translation because the
audience knew the originals – Russians often put us to shame
by the ease with which they hold in their minds great swathes
of poetry, while we in the West may have to struggle to
remember a few lines. A Russian poetry reading is as much
recital as actual reading. So it was on the occasion – Aygi read
from books, to be sure, but at the same time he was plunging
into his memory and holding the audience enthralled by his
intense meditation on the verse he offered them.

People had come from far away, from Scotland, from St
Petersburg, and from Aygi's native land, Chuvashia, some 500

miles away to the east among the snowy plains of central Russia. For these people poetry mattered. And the importance of poetry was demonstrated again a month later when the poet's body was taken from Moscow to Cheboksary, the Chuvash capital, where the country's president paid a moving tribute to their national poet, who was taken the following day to his last resting place in his native village. He was buried in the graveyard at the edge of the village, surrounded by the white snowy fields which are a central point of reference in his work. Those present will have recalled one of his early poems, on the death of his mother, which ends:

> Oh, how quiet the snows,
> as if smoothed by the wings
> of yesterday's demon.
>
> Oh, how rich the drifts,
> as if they concealed
> mountains of heathen
>
> sacrificial offerings.
>
> But the snowflakes
> keep carrying carrying earthwards
>
> the hieroglyphs of god . . .

He was buried close to his mother and his maternal grandfather, the latter a peasant who was also the last pagan priest of the village. Aygi himself was often called a 'shaman' – he declined the term, but for him poetry was a 'sacred rite' whose role was to maintain human solidarity – and the solidarity of humanity with the natural world. Acutely aware as he was of the passing of the old communal culture – emblematised by the choral dance of the Chuvash – he worked to 'preserve human warmth under the cold sky of the world'.

Friendship and brotherhood were vital in his work, so it was appropriate that he translated into Chuvash some poems of Robert Burns and helped to set up a Burns event in Chuvashia in 1996. Similarly, he had translated into his native tongue poems by a number of modern Scottish poets, Hugh MacDiarmid, Edwin Morgan and several more – a contribution to what was intended as a Chuvash anthology of Scottish poetry. This was a gesture of reciprocity, since the work of translating into English his own remarkable *Anthology of Chuvash Poetry* had been done by me in Scotland (I worked from Russian versions that he himself had made). His first visit to Britain was to Scotland, where he laid earth from a Chuvash graveyard on the steps of the Burns mausoleum.

Aygi's versions of Scottish poetry were only a small part of his translation work. Like many poets in the Soviet Union (including his beloved master, Pasternak), he had been able to subsist as a writer partly on his earnings as a translator. In his case, given the importance accorded to the cultures of the different Soviet 'nationalities', this meant translating into his native Chuvash, first from what had become his own first poetic language, Russian, but then from several other European languages. In particular, having learned French at the Moscow Literary Institute in order to read Baudelaire in the original, he produced an extraordinary Chuvash anthology of French poetry from François Villon to Yves Bonnefoy, with a generous representation of modern poets such as Max Jacob, René Char or Pierre-Jean Jouve. These poets meant a lot to him personally, but they also revolutionised Chuvash poetry by revealing to his compatriots new poetic possibilities. So while some of his translation work was done to earn a living, much of it had a different function: to bring together far-distant writers and readers and to bring new riches to the land-locked culture of his own small nation.

As well as translating into Chuvash, he worked to spread the Chuvash word abroad. The Chuvash people, speaking a Turkic language, have preserved much of their own culture and relics of their old religion in the face of centuries of Russification. It was Aygi's belief that 'small peoples' such as his had their word to say in the concert of nations, an important word that larger, more confident cultures would be unwise to ignore. To this end he devoted many years to creating an anthology of Chuvash poetry, from ancient pagan prayers, through folksongs and ethnographic descriptions of festivals, to poetry of the late twentieth century. This was to be his country's 'visiting card' to the rest of the world, and thanks largely to UNESCO it now exists in many languages. (Interestingly, the English-language version published by Forest Books in 1991 was reviewed in *Verse* alongside the reissue of Alexander Carmichael's famous collection of Gaelic folk poetry, *Carmina Gadelica*.)

Aygi translated a great deal then, but as a Russian poet he has in his turn been much translated. The story of his worldwide reception is an exemplary one. As a young poet, growing up in a remote village, he naturally wrote in Chuvash, but his father had been a Russian teacher and quite early on he discovered modern poetry through the Russian poetry of Mayakovsky. On being 'talent-spotted' and sent to the Literary Institute in Moscow, he found himself in a Russian-speaking milieu, and began to translate his Chuvash poems into Russian. But it was above all the persuasion of Boris Pasternak, a master, friend and neighbour, and of the Turkish poet Nazim Hikmet that determined him to move to writing in Russian – the very first poem written directly in that language being the poem on his mother's death quoted above. So while he continued to translate into Chuvash, as a poet he now belonged to a great culture which plugged him in more directly to the modern art and literature of the whole world.

At the same time, unfortunately, he was cut off from Russian readers. His friendship with Pasternak (at the time of the Nobel affair) and his own highly unorthodox poetics made him persona non grata with the cultural establishment, and virtually none of his Russian poetry was published in the Soviet Union until the late 1980s. He said in an interview he gave in

1985: 'For over twenty years I had fewer than a dozen readers' – a small circle of like-minded artists and writers.

Meanwhile, though, from as early as 1962, his work began to appear outside Russia. The very first poems were translations by his Polish friend Wiktor Woroszylski. These were noticed by the German translator Karl Dedecius, who in 1971 published with Suhrkamp his own Aygi volume, *Beginn der Lichtung* – and before this there had also been volumes in Czech and Slovak. By 1980 translations had appeared in many countries, notably France, where Léon Robel worked tirelessly to bring Aygi to the attention of French poets and readers, and Germany, where Felix Philipp Ingold assumed the mantle of Dedecius, publishing numerous volumes, including a two-volume *Ausgewählte Werke* (1995-98). The first English translations, by Robin Milner-Gulland, figure in the 1977 Penguin *Russian Writing Today*; they were quickly followed by translations by Edwin Morgan and myself, and there have subsequently been six books in English in addition to the Chuvash anthology.

We have therefore the situation, by no means unique in modern times, of a poet being better known abroad than at home, and this above all through translation. Of course there were also Russian-language publications of his work outside the Soviet Union, both Russian-only editions and bilingual volumes, but I think it is fair to say that these were carried along on the wave of translation. This state of affairs did not endear Aygi to the authorities at home. The publication of some of his poems (in Russian) in the Paris émigré journal *Kontinent* in 1975 brought him considerable harassment in Chuvashia – for many years he was unable to travel from Moscow to his native land. And in more recent years, as he has been increasingly recognized and published in post-perestroika Russia and Chuvashia, there have been those who have sought to cast doubt on his achievement, portraying him as a poet for foreigners. It may indeed be true that Aygi's free verse, with its highly original punctuation and creative use of type-face and

layout, is more easily assimilated in the West, and particularly
in France, than in the still quite traditional poetic culture of
Russia. But this is only to say that through his creative reading
of some of the masterworks of modern poetry he has been able
to bring something new to the poetry of Russia. His poetry is
world poetry, perhaps, but it is in no sense rootless, burrowing
deep into the resources and sonorities of the Russian language.
His themes and leitmotif images – snow, field, forest, flowers,
but also pain and grief – are both Russian and Chuvash, as in
the short and mysterious poem of 1981, 'To an Icon of the
Mother of God', which I also read in translation on the evening
of January 17 (I have kept something of the neologisms of the
original, but not the beauty of sound):

in dreamings and visionings
in dawn day of nonevening
in the house blazing with coals
benedissolution
of joygrieving!
in a corner-sanctuary that as with heart's coals
in dreamings and visionings
as if amid the field the Living
to the abandoned feasting table
like signs many assembled

This is difficult poetry, and many will not easily accept it, in
Russia as elsewhere, but it does seem now that as well as being
for the last twelve years the Chuvash national poet, Gennady
Aygi has found his place in the canon of Russian poetry.
Meanwhile his career as a translated poet of the world will
continue. Translation brought him many honours – and in the
last eighteen years much travel – but above all it has helped
create a network of friends/readers all round the world who
can share through his poetry a universal vision that is still
grounded in the distant fields and forests of the Chuvash land.
Let me finish, by way of a tribute, with a valedictory sequence

from his *Salute – to Singing,* a collection of a hundred quatrains, variations in Russian on Chuvash and other folksongs:

The village is long since out of sight,
but the windows in our father's house
whistle through cracks in the frame,
calling us home again.

Mother, you will start sweeping the room,
and remembering me, perhaps,
you will stop short
by the door and burst out crying.

A candle burns,
unseen by the red fox's eye,
farewell – my young soul's features
will abide among you.

Enough, we have swung and swung
like resounding silver coins,
we shall bow, we shall bend before you,
like paper money, all white.

And where we stood,
may there remain
the shining of our
benediction.

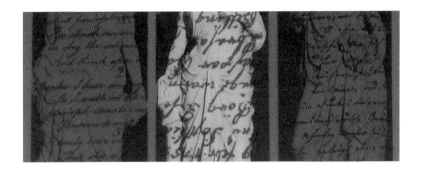

Francis R. Jones
Stroking hands over the heart: ten translators and the verse of Gerrit Kouwenaar

Processes and poems

Poetry translators strive to copy an original ('source') poem perfectly into another ('target') language. This, of course, is impossible, because a poem is deeply and complexly embedded in its own language. Hence they have to settle for the possible, for a compromise between the instructions given by the source poem and the opportunities of the target language. But whereas all copies are alike, all compromises are different – not only in the target poem that translators produce, but also in the processes that lead to that product. A workshop on translating Gerrit Kouwenaar, the elder grand master of Dutch poetry, gave an opportunity to chart these working processes, how they differ, and how the differences between them might be harnessed. This is the topic of this article.

The legacy of James Brockway, a lifelong translator and tireless ambassador of Dutch poetry in English, has sponsored a biennial Prize and Workshop for the translation of Dutch poetry. The first Brockway Workshop, in June 2005, focused on translating recent work by Gerrit Kouwenaar into English. Organised by Thomas Möhlmann of the Foundation for the Production and Translation of Dutch Literature (NLPVF) and chaired by poet Erik Menkveld and myself, it gathered together nine working translators of poetry: David Colmer, Diane Butterman-Dorey, Karlien van den Beukel, Lloyd Haft, Paul Evans, Paul Vincent, Renée Delhez, Susan Massotty and Willem Groenewegen. Kouwenaar answered translators' questions in one afternoon session, and input also came from publishers Christopher MacLehose, Robert Minhinnick and Tony Ward. In the workshop's five days, just seven poems were worked on, all from Kouwenaar's recent work.

Gerrit Kouwenaar

In many ways, these poems are typical of Gerrit Kouwenaar's long oeuvre. Like earlier works, they show a concern with memory, the sense of a ghostly past held present while the poem lasts. And they show his old mastery of Dutch. Thus the poem 'toen wij' begins 'Toen wij onze handen over ons hart streken' – literally, 'When we stroked our hands over our heart'. This refers to the Dutch idiom 'to stroke one's hand over one's heart', which means 'to show compassion'. But Kouwenaar also reanimates its literal meaning, as a gesture of love: I stroked your heart, and you mine. The reanimated semantics of 'heart' then serves to awaken the literal, sensual meanings of two idioms in the next line, 'weet jij nog hoe het klopte' – idiomatically 'do you remember how it was right', but literally 'do you still know how it was beating'. Kouwenaar also still shows his old mystery of meaning. Who are 'we', for example? And why this sense of erotic grace?

Kouwenaar's tone and topics are darker than in his earlier verse, however. These poems tell of contemporaries dead, such as the poet Lucebert. Or of how his small house in France, the setting of the poem just mentioned, now holds only the ghost of his wife, as his own 'mortal light' is about to dim.

Translating these poems was a challenge. But responding to this challenge had a triple benefit. It convinced all at the workshop that it was high time for a full volume of Kouwenaar's work to be assembled in English – a task which fell naturally to Lloyd Haft, as the poet's long-standing English translator. Responding to this challenge also gave invaluable insights both into Kouwenaar's work and into the nature of poetry translation. For the former, I refer the English reader to the Rotterdam Poetry International website*. This essay focuses on three aspects of the latter: translators' working priorities, their working processes, and how differences between translators can be harnessed in collaborative translating.

Talking translation

The workshop participants translated three poems beforehand as starting-points for discussion. Discussions based on these poems took no fewer than one and a half days. The direction of discussions was largely set by translators themselves. This allowed the choice of topics to open a window onto the key concerns of poetry translators.

Most talk-time by far was taken up with problems of meaning and equivalence. In other words, working out exactly what the source poet means by the words and phrases in the poem, and then the best single target-language equivalent, seems central to how poetry translators see their task. What, for instance, does Kouwenaar mean in the poem 'alleen in de tuin' ('alone in the garden') when he follows 'men zou dit ingedikt niets willen stillen' (literally, 'one would want to appease this condensed nothing') with 'ontmaken / deze langzame cirkel'? Susan Massotty, in her pre-workshop draft, translated the latter clause literally as 'undo / this slow circle' – seeing the circle as a metaphor for life, perhaps. A word,

*http://netherlands.poetryinternationalweb.org/piw_cms/cms/
ms_module/index.php?obj_id=4009

however, is usually a bundle of several related meanings, and different languages almost always bundle their meanings slightly differently. This means that there is rarely even one literal English equivalent for a Dutch word. With 'ontmaken', say, this leaves the relative merits of 'undo' and 'unmake' open to debate – never mind the fact that the allusion(s) given off by a word may make translators consider a solution that stresses the allusive rather than the literal meaning. And in questions of cross-language problems and solutions, there are no more eager debaters than translators. In our case, the poet could later explain what he actually meant here. He said that 'ontmaken / deze langzame cirkel' alluded to rewinding a reel-to-reel tape. This led Paul Vincent to revise this phrase into 'unmake / this slow-turning loop'.

But this links to an issue raised during discussions: do translators *need* to understand every last detail and implication, or should they simply translate what the poem seems to say on the surface? Or, to put it differently, should insider information gained from the poet's mouth always out-trump what the translator sees in the text as a reader? In the end, we felt there was no clear answer. Hence, in my view, Massotty's and Vincent's versions succeed in different ways. 'Undo / this slow circle', for example, is a crystalline translation that combines exactness, concision and alliterative force. By contrast, 'unmake / this slow-turning loop' creates a powerful poetic image that sheds a different light on Kouwenaar's original, but without explaining away its mystery.

Translators think aloud

These issues, of course, were raised by translators when they were not translating. But what are their concerns *whilst* they translate? To answer questions such as this, I and four volunteers from the workshop participants took part in a so-called 'think-aloud' study while translating the poem 'toen wij' mentioned earlier. This involved each of us translating the poem solo, while giving a running commentary into a cassette recorder about everything that we were thinking and doing. Translating poetry typically involves several revisions, with between them what Flaubert called the crucial time 'in the drawer'. Hence each translator was recorded translating and revising the poem over three separate sessions, during a period of several weeks centred on the workshop itself.

But what do the tapes reveal about poetry translating as a process? Most striking is the sheer amount of time translators spend translating poetry. The first two drafts of this 11-line poem typically took an hour and a half each, though most third drafts were somewhat shorter. Moreover, two translators explicitly stated that they would normally produce more drafts before publication.

It is also clear, despite the impression given in the discussions, that relatively little translating time is spent on establishing meaning. This is simply the foundation of the English poem, which is laid down fairly quickly in the first draft. Far more time is spent redrafting, typically clause by clause: scrutinising, reciting, altering and rewriting. Crucial in redrafting is the translators' engagement with poetic image. Working out what 'buiten / de kleine kou van het najaar' (literally, 'outside / the small cold of the autumn') might actually *mean*, for example, and how the image it generates could be reproduced in English. Or if it cannot be reproduced, how a new image could be created that stays loyal to the underlying intent which the translator gets from the source poem (or poet) – 'outside / autumn hinted at winter', perhaps, as in one translator's version? No less crucial, however, is a focus in all drafts on the best way to word these images in English. Should one create more assonance by following 'outside / the small chill' with 'fall', say, even though the rest of the poem is in British English (leading the reader to expect 'autumn')? And after one pass through the text, translators go back to the beginning and starting all over again, and again. If we compare this data with similar studies on non-literary translation, one can confidently say that no other genre in translation gets anything near the intense amount of revision given to poetry.

As for what specific aspects of the poem took up most translating time, here differences emerged. Kouwenaar often 'unpacks' an idiom so that both its literal and its figurative meanings are alive in the poem, for example – as in 'when we stroked our hands over our heart' mentioned earlier. A reasonable hypothesis might be: when the same idiom does not exist in the target language, translators spend a lot of time tackling this problem. This was indeed generally the case – but not always. One translator spent about three quarters of an hour in Draft 2 trying to find an English phrase that meant 'showing compassion' using the words 'hand(s)' and 'heart' – brainstorming, searching through idiom dictionaries, Googling, or simply staring at the page. Another found it problematic enough to e-mail a fellow-translator and ask him for advice. A third translator showed that he experienced this phrase as problematic by the frequent and drastic changes he made in his target version. His first version 'when we took heart' soon changed to 'when our hearts were in our mouths'. This was before Kouwenaar's explanation, in the question-and-answer session, that the phrase showed his and his wife's sense of relief once they had bought their small French farmhouse. Following this clue, the translator later changed his rendering to 'when we took the plunge' – and this changed twice more before the end of the third session. A fourth translator spent a lot of time in Draft 2 tackling this and the following line (also mentioned earlier) as one unit, eventually putting the second image first: 'Do you remember how light it felt when we passed / our hands over our heart'. The fifth translator, however, spent relatively little time on the hands-heart problem.

All translators, however, spent some time identifying and solving rhythm and word-sound problems – typically in just one draft. All spoke the lines of both the source and target rhythmically. One translator counted and wrote down the number of syllables. Another, the translator most concerned with sound (25% of problem-solving time in Draft 3), used assonance as a way out of the idiom problem mentioned above: 'when hands on heart we felt it unharden'.

Translators also differed in the amount of research they did before translating. Some analysed the poem carefully, looked up key words and made extensive notes; others simply read the poem out loud once. When actually translating, some translators liked to fill their first drafts full of alternatives. These gave a bank of possibilities to choose from later:

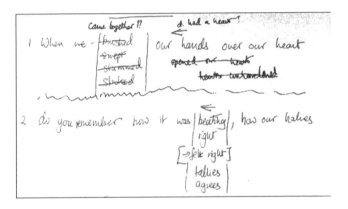

Others, however, aimed for a single 'pure line' from the beginning, if necessary by copying the draft out again as soon as it risked looking messy. The aim here, it seems, is to be able to judge how well the draft works as an English poem straight away:

In how translators pre-analysed and wrote down their drafts, we see echoes of differences noted for all sorts of mental tasks. Here, people can be seen as falling along a spectrum between the holists, who prefer to tackle tasks as a single, inter-connected whole, and the analysts, who prefer to break tasks down into details and tackle the details one at a time. Some people, of course, fall in between – which is why not every translator who did extensive pre-analysis had a lots-of-alternatives drafting style.

Translation as teamwork

As well as discussing the pre-translated poems and (for some) doing think-alouds, participants worked in three groups on a poem each. Despite occasional disagreement about tactics, workshop participants said they found it enriching to work closely with others. As Renée Delhez put it, 'you complement each other, are stimulated by the other's ideas and end up with a satisfying result, although of course you have to compromise a bit on your own 'finds' now and again' (my translation).

Anyway, interviews I have carried out with other translators show that poetry translators rarely work alone. This is backed up by translators' reports, such as those collected in Daniel Weissbort's *Translating Poetry: The Double Labyrinth**. One reason is that poetry translation is fiendishly complex, involving a combination of skills rarely found in one person – having an educated native reader's insight into the source text, say, whilst being a native writer of poetry in your target language. It is hardly surprising, therefore, that poetry translators often rely on colleagues and other experts to check over their drafts for the inevitable misinterpretations and stumbles in their own poetic line. And it is also quite common for poetry translators to work in partnership, typically a

*Published by Macmillan, 1989.

source-language and target-language native. The advantages of this, again in my translation of Delhez's words, are that

> two translators, each with their own background, in this case Dutch and English, can complement each other: no matter how good someone's command of both languages, the translator will still always have the best sense for the very subtlest nuances in his own language.

But if, as the think-alouds show, translators' working processes are different, collaborative translating may allow these differences to complement each other. The interviews I mentioned earlier suggested that poetry translators have different personalities, which can again be seen as different positions on a spectrum. At one extreme we have the 'word-smith', who works analytically and aims to be faithful to the original poem's imagery and feel. At the other extreme we have the 'jazz player', who works by holistic feel, and who sees it as important to convey the music of the text. In between we have the 'tightrope artists', who try to balance both. In my admittedly subjective view, this combining of translator personalities may be why the Colmer, Evans and Groenewegen version of '10 May 1994' succeeds so well as an English poem whilst reflecting the texture and nuances of the original:

> Heard this evening of your death at an hour
> that peace had almost descended on the day
>
> [Vanavond gehoord van je dood op een uur
> dat de dag haast stilstond van vrede]

Similarly, whether because of complementary first languages, complementary translator personalities or both, the Butterman-Dorey, Van den Beukel, Haft and Massotty version of 'in the orchard' convinces in English, without a stumble:

Poet, here I am again, jolted
awake in you, I'm walking with you
through the stilled future of our past

This, of course, is also an outstanding original poem, in which the grand master of Dutch poetry unflinchingly confronts his dead muse, bringing him and us face to face with our own mortality:

poet, nothing rhymes with dead, I caress
the decaying velvet of my nightdress, go back
to sleep, in you

This version, to my mind, fulfils Robert Graves's definition of true poetry: that it makes the hairs stand on end in the knowledge that we are in the presence of the Muse, the White Goddess. And it alters Robert Frost's definition from 'poetry is what is lost in translation' to 'poetry is what gets through in good translation'.

Acknowledgments

Many thanks to the translators for letting me discuss and quote their poems, to the translators and Thomas Möhlmann for their feedback on this article, and to Paul Vincent and Renée Delhez for their comments on the workshop. With particular thanks to Willem Groenewegen for letting me refer to his detailed diary report on the workshop. I am grateful to the British Academy for a Small Research Grant which enabled the think-aloud tapes to be transcribed and analysed – and to Dimitris Asimakoulas for his work on the analysis.

Reviews

Yang Lian
Concentric Circles
Translated by Brian Holton and Agnes Hung-Chong Chan
Bloodaxe Books
ISBN 1-85224-703-7
Pb. 111 pages. £8.95

Wings of Summer: Selected Poems of Zheng Danyi 1984–1997
Translated by Luo Hui
Sixth Finger Press
ISBN 9- 8897051 9
Hardback, 336pp. £19

Yang Lian's *Concentric Circles* and Zheng Danyi's *Wings of Summer* exemplify two generations of contemporary Chinese poets as well as two very different approaches to translation and publication. Yang Lian, a prominent member of the Misty School with a worldwide reputation, is represented here in an edition aimed at the English-reading market. Zheng Danyi's bilingual publication is for Chinese as well as English readers, making available, for the first time, a substantial number of poems that, if not widely translated, has long had an underground following.

Yang Lian, a poet with long experience of exile, is aware of translation as a two-way process, shaped by expectations and counter-expectations. In his introduction to *Concentric Circles*, he wonders whether an English version 'compelled to make clear the person of verbs and choose their tense, as well as define nouns as singular or plural, will open the sealed magic box, or break an exquisite piece of porcelain'. Happily, his conclusion is that Holton and Hung-Chong Chan's work is a 'new beginning', a place where its assumptions and workings can be tested and placed under pressure in a spirit of adventure, even risk.

Following Yang Lian's interest in the spatial and typographical possibilities of Chinese, Holton and Hung-Chong Chan use mainly unpunctuated and uncapitalized English arranged in spaced blocks. The original structure of the book – horizontally into ever-widening circles (represented graphically in the text by using a series of depictions of concentric circles instead of chapter numbers) and vertically into what Yang Lian calls 'multi-storey' spaces – is preserved, representing its underlying themes: space, place and 'the pain of timelessness'.

While there are clearly autobiographical elements here, Yang Lian distinguishes between these and the 'abstract' sections that surround them. Here, exile, diaspora, the aftermath of the pro-democracy movement, are not final terms. Just as classical Chinese and Chinese history continue to be ongoing presences in Chinese culture, so the culture of diasporic China co-exists with 'the mainland'. Similarly the square shapes of Chinese characters provide a powerful metaphor for a set of synchronous Chinese realities, changing and unchanging at the same time.

For example, the final chapter in the book (identified by five concentric circles) is based on the Chinese character for poetry, and is subdivided into the three graphic elements of that

character, in English 'talking', 'earth' and 'inch'. Each of these
is then used to generate a series of sub-poems with, in the case
of 'talking', titles such as 'questioning', 'lies', and 'obituary'.
All three sections of the chapter end with a reprise, 'Poetry',
that echoes images used within the section, tying the chapter
together. These reprise poems read vertically on the page as
well as horizontally, a reminder of how Chinese itself is often
read. For example, the final one, the last poem in *Concentric
Circles*, opens

nil
    vanishing to three
word
    three autumns go over the border
far
    three times toward the light birds radiate medicinal shadows
from
    Dante is the one refused by a key
it-
    vanishing is thought
self's
    what can't be redeemed stows away to form the next line.

Pound's influence is obvious, as Yang Lian acknowledges in
his introduction, arguing that his own *Concentric Circles* and
Holton and Hung-Chong Chan's translation perform a kind
of cross-cultural dialogue between the *Cantos* (especially in
Chinese translation) and Chinese poetry. The implications of
this for the translation process are discussed by Holton and
Hung-Chong Chan in an informative afterword. Here we
discover some of their radical approaches to poems whose
structures are almost purely sonic or graphic. A poem
originally titled 'Shei' ('Who' in Chinese), for example, a
Chinese pure-sound poem using a traditional form based on
patterns of tones becomes 'Sway', a near-homophonic rendering
in English monosyllables (mainly) written in a Welsh bardic

metre. Other creative solutions include the use of Greek (transcribed into the Latin alphabet) for a poem written in archaic Seal Script characters, and a parody of Augustan English for a poem written in a parody of the style of the Han dynasty historian Ban Gu.

Zheng Danyi's *Wings of Summer* also shows a writer who is interested in pushing at linguistic boundaries, but his translator admits to a more conservative approach, suggesting in his introduction that the lyricism and 'flowing exuberance' of Zheng's style may present challenges to English readers looking for 'terseness'. Indeed, the parallel poems encourage the reader to compare the somewhat short English lines on the right-hand page with the more fluid Chinese on the left. Here Zheng can be seen to be a master of rhythm and pacing, as the Chinese characters combine, separate, repeat, perform line- and stanza-break enjambments.

Luo Hui's translations give a clear mapping of the images in Zheng's poems and their positioning stanza by stanza. As the title of the collection suggests, much of the work uses natural imagery, which, as in 'Spring', gives the poetry a formidable intensity through both sound and emotional association. Themes and mood are wide-ranging. Alongside the bitterness and plangency of the work in 'Sixteen Poems' (a series written in 1989, whose first publication, shortly after Tiananmen, was heavily censored) is delicate love poetry, as for example in the title poem: 'I . . . see you, wings folded in a loose shirt / Walking on my clean floor. Evening breezes are gentle / And cool, in a place autumn wind does not reach'.

Putting these two collections side by side highlights the way in which poetry in Chinese seems to push to an extreme the translator's dilemma — caught between sound-pattern, meaning-pattern and eye-pattern. Luo Hui mentions Zheng Danyi's 'electric' readings: an additional CD slipped into the back page would have been welcome. Foot-notes, too, could have offered powerful tools for exploring the cross-cultural dynamics and complex architectures of Yang Lian's work.

Poetry, especially poetry moving between languages, is always
so much more than ink on the inside surfaces of a book . . .

Anna Reckin

Clive Scott
Translating Rimbaud's Illuminations
University of Exeter Press
ISBN 0-85989-769-9
pb 328pp. £15.99

Ruth Fainlight
Moonwheels
Bloodaxe Books
ISBN 1-85224-742-8
pb 111pp. £8.95

Alexei Sayle once said that he went to Chelsea Art School to
become good at drawing horses and pillar boxes, not to
confront reality by wearing a teapot on his head: Clive Scott's
Translating Rimbaud's Illuminations is for those of us prepared to
go with the teapot. Daunting in its scholarship (a must for
postgraduate translation courses) and quite magically mad in
its attempts to merge theory and practice, Scott himself expects
his ideas to give rise to 'irritated scepticism or exasperated
disbelief at times'. He achieves the opposite however: his
enthusiasm, his clarity in the face of complex ideas, the
intelligence and thoroughness of his research (providing an
excellent bibliography) and the fun of engaging with the
wizardry of his experimental translations all carry the reader
along.
    Taking Rimbaud's prose poems as his context Scott argues

that the purpose of translation is not to provide a 'definitive' poem for those unfamiliar with the language but to reflect the translator's encounter with the poem: 'the reading experience itself, the fluctuations of associations, intertextual memory, modality, function, context'. The solution is experimental writing with 'the space of the page as the translator's mental landscape, or imaginative territory'. Scott provides an in-depth discussion of acoustics, silence and space, drawing on his wide knowledge of linguistics, literary theory and the visual arts, and his own translations to illustrate his argument.

The discussions are all sound and thought-provoking: the resulting translations are in most cases (apart from some rather beautiful montages of Rimbaud's city poems) impossible to grasp without accompanying commentary, and that is where the fun begins. Take his discussion of resonant silence. Scott opens with the copyright court case between Cage and Batt over two 'identical' pieces of silent music – Batt's defence: 'Ours is a better silence: it's digital. Theirs is only analogue.' It is also pointed out that Batt's piece is in the key of G. This, of course, is all a hoot, but then, as the laughter dies down, Scott quite rationally points out:

silence is not an acoustic blank, but has specific resonances, specific motives, specific generical possibilities—the silence of romance (fear of breaking a spell or an image by speaking, by uttering a banality, or activating a non-euphonic voice) is a far cry from the silence of the thriller (stealth, resistance, bluff)....

All well and good, but then how does Scott convey this? Read on:

———————————-and the
pleasure x x / x))))) of this so special
**************décor ! !!!!! ! and time of day 00 oo .....
.>>>> (((((.

All is made clear when we have the key with its seven types of silence, such as:

(((())   acoustic reverberations and their directions
>>>>   impatience to read on
***   a certain erotic charge
^^^   psychosomatic reaction

It's worth getting this text for the entertainment value in the sheer invention of the varied translations and their extensive commentaries; it's also worth it for Scott's convincingly argued belief that:

> The translator belongs to a literary community in which a collage of voices occupies a collective space, so that literary ownership is constantly being transferred.

Back in the eighties Ruth Fainlight wrote: 'Writing poetry is what I do to make contact with my spirit and the spirits that inhabit me.' *Moonwheels*, with its thirty new poems, reprints from two earlier collections and a variety of translations, provides a fine showcase of her work, with clear evidence of this spiritual process. At times, her poems are reminiscent of a Mike Leigh play – beings who seem to inhabit a mundane world of platitudes but are in fact engaged in a struggle with the human condition. She states in 'Thunder': 'Half/ of my nature is simple as a medieval/ peasant. The other isn't, and that's the problem.' She also sees this paradox in others, as in 'Romance': 'Smoothing his shirts, she dreamed/ of transformation and reward . . .' She lets the reader in on her meditative processes, so we end up somewhere completely different from where we started out, as in the shocking conceptual leap of 'Crocuses':

shivering petals the almost luminous
blue and mauve of bruises on the naked

bodies of men, women, children
herded into a forest clearing . . .

She has the knack of creating a fierce shock of recognition
when she captures the uniqueness of an ordinary action as in 'A
Mourner':

I put my head on my arms on my desk
to weep, and the smell and heat of my breath
remind me of afternoons at school
when the teacher made us stop our noise
and running around, and take a rest.

Not since then, except in love's
embrace, have the damp intensities
of my own body and feelings so
combined.

But again we are being led by the hand, for the power of the
image is such that we momentarily forget the title's import
and have to be reminded: 'In all the confusion/ and turmoil,
there should be a mourner.' Throughout the collection we see
Fainlight teasing out meaning from the patterns and minutiae
of the physical world.

This volume also provides ample examples of Fainlight's
beautifully seamless translations, most notably of the Peruvian
poet César Vallejo and, from Portuguese, Sophia de Mello
Breyner, Maria Negroni (Argentina), as well as Elsa Cross and
Victor Manuel Mendiola (Mexico). Fainlight gives cohesion
to *Moonwheels* by providing translations with similar
epistemological subject matter. She has already translated two
collections of de Mello Breyner's poetry and the examples here

might whet one's appetite to seek out those collections. Take, for example, 'Muse':

> Muse teach me the song
> Of the sea's breath
> . . .
> So I can say
> How evening there
> Touched door and table
> Cup and mirror
> How it embraced . . .

Vallejo offers us powerfully moving lines like: 'We should always be leaving. We should savour/ that splendid song, song murmured/ by the under-lips of longing.' Similarly, the Mexican poet Elsa Cross, like Fainlight, scans the physical world for meaning:

> She seeks out the angle
> where the ray of sunlight
> touches the eye's surface
> and plays at reflection ...

Both Fainlight's and Scott's texts can be thoroughly recommended: for where Scott provides plenty to challenge the brain, Fainlight offers something to renew the soul.

Belinda Cooke

Shorter Reviews: Middle- and Far-Eastern Round-Up

Kawamura Bunichiro *The Midday of Substances*, edited and translated by Kumagai Yuriya J., Schichosha Publishing, 171pp, hardback, ISBN 4-7837-1958-6.

A bi-lingual edition of the influential Japanese poet, with lively translations by Professor Kumagai. As Kumagai explains in her informative introduction, Kawamura's final work, written in New York during and immediately after 9/11, is included here and makes for powerful reading, linking the tragedy with that of the allied bombing of Japan in 1945.

Yihai Chen, *Song of Simone & Seven Sad Songs*, Heaventree Press, 44pp, paperback, £5, ISBN 0-9458811-6-8.

Poems composed and translated by Chinese poet Yihai Chen during a visiting scholarship at the Centre for Translation and Comparative Studies at Warwick University in 2005. 'Translation', 'Lost in Translation' and 'Thirteen Approaches to Languages' are witty, bitter-sweet musings on the difficulties of moving between languages and cultures: indispensable reading.

Po Chü- I, *Selected Poems*, translated by David Hinton, Anvil Press, 224pp, paperback, £12.95, ISBN 0-85646-335-3.

Beautiful and sparse, David Hinton's masterful translations bring a wide selection of the ninth-century AD Chinese poet's work to English-speaking readers for the first time.

Pak Chaesam, *Enough to Say It's Far: Selected Poems*, translated by David R. McCann and Jiwon Shin, Princeton, 152pp, paperback, £9.95, ISBN 0-691-12446-9.

The first English translations of the South Korean poet in a bi-lingual edition with translators' introductions. Mysterious and sensual.

Bei Dao, *Unlock,* Translated by Eliot Weinberger & Iona Man-Cheong, Anvil Press, 128pp, paperback, £8.95, ISBN 0-85646-336-1.

A new bi-lingual edition of the sixth collection by the now-exiled leading Chinese poet and conscience of the Democracy Movement. Beautifully translated by Eliot Einberger in collaboration with historian Iona Man-Cheong and Bei Dao himself, this is an important work for all those interested not just in modern Chinese affairs but poetry itself. A Poetry Book Society Recommended Translation.

Said, *The Place I Die I Shall Not Belong,* translated by Laurence James, Lapwing Publications, 32pp, paperback, ISBN 1-905425-26-0.

The exiled Iranian writer Said was awarded this year's Goethe Prize for his work in his adopted German language, although it is little-known in Britain. Here poet and translator Laurence James provides very welcome versions of Said's 1983 collection, a moving and important meditation on the exile's journey to his new homeland.

Love's Alchemy: Poems from the Sufi Tradition, translated from the Persian by David and Sabrineh Fideler, New World Library, 213pp, hardback, $18, ISBN 1-57731-535-9.

A lovely edition covering all major poets of the Sufi tradition, including Rumi, with helpful introduction, glossary and explanatory notes. Unlike many English versions, which rely on interpreting other English editions, the Fidelers have gone back to the Persian texts to produce reliable, as well as accessible translations of these deceptively simple verses.

Michael Bullock, *Moons and Mirrors*, translated into Chinese by Jenny Tse and K.L. Leung, Wah Hon Publishing, 160pp, paperback, $15, ISBN 962-288-123-8.

A bi-lingual edition of Michael Bullock's sparse but lyrical verse, itself influenced by Chinese poetry, here translated into Chinese script and calligraphy by Jenny Tse, with the help of Professor K.L. Leung. It's a surprisingly affecting exercise. As Bullock notes: 'looking at my poems in Chinese is like gazing at a beautiful but opaque curtain behind which is someone I know but cannot see.'

Lee Kuei-shien, *Between Islands*, translated by Simon Patton, Pacific View Press, paperback, 64pp, ISBN 1-881896-28-5, $17.95

An excellent introduction to the veteran Taiwanese poet, who was nominated for a Nobel Prize for literature in 2002 and is a founder member of Taiwanese PEN. Lee's delicate, luminous poetry is well-served by translator Simon Patton, who also provides a thoughtful – and helpful – translator's introduction. Well worth seeking out.

Ko Un, *Ten Thousand Lives*, translated by Brother Anthony of Taizé, Young-moo Kim and Gary Gach, Green Integer 123, 364pp, paperback, $14.95, ISBN 1-933382-06-6.

Korean poet Ko Un became a Buddhist monk in 1952 and began writing *Ten Thousand Lives* whilst imprisoned in the mid 1950s, with the aim of describing in verse every person he had ever met. Now in its 20th volume in Korean, this handy pocket-sized English edition, with a helpful introduction by Robert Hass, offers selections from the work's first ten volumes – and a cornucopia of characters, from the poet's family to fellow villagers, travelling peddlers and passing acquaintances. Life-affirming

A Waka Anthology: Volume Two: Grasses of Remembrance, translated with commentary, appendices, and notes by Edward A Cranston, Stanford University Press, 688pp, hardback, $175, ISBN 0-8047-4825-X.
Professor Cranston's scholarly edition concentrates on Japanese court poetry from A.D. 890-1080, with over 2,600 poems in translation, including all the poems from *The Tale of the Genji*. Each poem is introduced by a brief explanatory note and is printed alongside a transcription of the original Japanese text.

Further Books Received:

New from Arc:
Juris Kronbergs, *Wolf One-Eye*, translated by Mara Rozitis/ introduced by Jaan Kaplinski, 132pp, paperback, £9.99, ISBN 1-904614-33-7.
Welcome versions of the Latvian poet's magical cycle of poems charting the adventures of his mythical protagonist.

Tomaz Šalamun, *Row*, translated and introduced by Joshua Beckman, 135pp, paperback, £9.99, ISBN 1-904614-09-4.
An English edition of the latest collection from the acclaimed Slovenian poet

New from Bloodaxe:
Neil Astley (ed), *Bloodaxe Poetry Introductions 2: Hans Magnus Enzensberger, Miroslav Holub, Marin Sorescu, Tomas Tranströmer*, 96 pages, paperback, £7.95, ISBN 1-85224-739-8.
Four of Europe's major poets in one volume, translated by some of Britain's finest translators including Ewald Osers and Michael Hamburger.

Tua Forsström, *I Studied Once at a Wonderful Faculty*, translated by David McDuff and Stina Katchadoourian, 136pp, paperback, £8.95, ISBN 1-85224-649-9.

A lovely edition of – and introduction to – the Finland-Swedish poet's incandescent poetry.

Miroslav Holub, *Poems Before and After: Collected English Translations* (new expanded edition), 440pp, paperback, £12, ISBN 1-85224-747-9.

An comprehensive collection of the renowned Czech poet's work covering over 40 years of his poetry from the 1950s to 1997. Essential reading for anyone interested in European literature, translation and, of course, poetry.

New from Carcanet:

Karen Leeder (ed), *After Brecht: A Celebration*, paperback, 110pp, ISBN 1-85754-883-3, £12.95

Published to mark the 50th anniversary of Brecht's death, *After Brecht* offers an intriguing anthology of 50 German poets – 'those who will live after' – including Paul Celan, Hans Magnus Enzensberger and Wolf Biermann, whose work commemorates, imitates, challenges and complements Brecht's own poetic legacy. These are all admirably served by an A-team of translators – Michael Hamburger, Michael Hofmann, David Constantine, Richard Dove as well as Leeder herself. As B.K. Tragelehn has it, in Leeder's translation: 'You the teachable teacher/Taught us learning./That is what remains'

Joachim Sartorius, *Ice Memory: Selected Poems*, edited by Richard Dove with an afterword by Christopher Middleton, 187pp, paperback, £12.95, ISBN 1-8574-832-9.

The first English edition of the German poet, with translations by Nathaniel Tarn, Michael Hamburger, Christopher Middleton, amongst others.

New from Five Leaves Publications:
Jennifer Langer (ed), *The Silver Throat of the Moon: Writing in Exile*, 325pp, paperback, £9.99, ISBN 0-907123-65-1.

A welcome sister volume to Langer's previous anthology, *The Bend in the Road*, with poetry and prose from around the globe, as well as series of essays on exile and writing in exile.

New from Libris Press:
Reiner Kunze and Mireille Gansel, *In Time of Need, A Conversation about Poetry, Resistance and Exile*, translated by Edmund Jephcott, with an essay on Peter Huchel by Ritchie Robertson, 120pp, hardback, £20, ISBN 1-870352-07-6.

A fascinating dialogue on the place of poetry and poets under Hitler and during the repressive years of the East German regime, centering on the life and work of Peter Huchel. This is a book with far-reaching relevance.

New from Penguin Classics:
Dante, *Inferno*, translated by Robin Kirkpatrick, 449pp, £10.99, ISBN 0-140-44895-0.

A major new translation, the first volume of Kirkpatrick's complete version of Dante's *Commedia* for Penguin Classics.

Books for review should be sent to Josephine Balmer, Reviews Editor, *Modern Poetry in Translation*, East Meon, St John's Road, Crowborough, East Sussex, TN6 1RW.

Acknowledgements, an Apology and a Correction

We owe particular thanks to Ruth Borthwick, Head of Literature and Talks at the South Bank Centre, for allowing us to be involved in the celebration of Brecht at this year's Poetry International; and to Naomi Jaffa, Director of the Aldeburgh Poetry Festival, for the poems of Joan Margarit and Durs Grünbein, who will be reading there.

The translations of the poems by Thomas Brasch are printed by kind permission of Suhrkamp Verlag; those of the poems and prose pieces by Brecht by kind permission of Stefan Brecht, who retains the copyright, and of Suhrkamp Verlag, and with particular acknowledgement of the edition of the new Herr Keuner material prepared by the head of the Brecht Archive, Erdmut Wizisla, *Geschichten vom Herrn Keuner. Zürcher Fassung* (Frankfurt a.M.: Suhrkamp 2004). Translations of the poems by Durs Grünbein are taken from *Ashes for Breakfast, Selected Poems of Durs Grünbein*, translated by Michael Hofmann, by kind permission of Faber and Faber Ltd.

We very much regret that in publishing Meles Negusse's 'Wild Animals' (in *MPT* 3/5) we omitted the name of Dr Ghirmai Negash as co-translator of that poem. Dr Negash is Assistant Director of the African Studies Program at Ohio University and co-author (with Charles Cantalupo) of *Who Needs a Story: Contemporary Eritrean Poetry in Tigrinya, Tigre and Arabic*.

In the footnote on p.170 of *MPT* 3/5, Richard Burns' collection is wrongly referred to as *The Messenger*. The correct title is *The Manager*.

Notes on Contributors

Tara Bergin was born in Dublin. Publications include *Russian Conversations* (Mudfog, 2005) and work in *Poetry Review* and *Northern Review*. Her short story *The Italian is not my Songbird* was recently broadcast on Radio 4.

Alison Brackenbury's most recent collection is *Bricks and Ballads* (Carcanet, 2004). New poems can be seen on her website, www.alisonbrackenbury.co.uk.

Tom Cheesman lectures in German at University of Wales Swansea. He established Hafan Books to publish writing by refugees and other poets in Wales. The latest anthology, bilingual, with Welsh translations mainly by Grahame Davies, takes its title from a poem by Adel Guémar: *Gwyl y Blaidd / The Festival of the Wolf* (co-published with Parthian, 2006). See www.hafan.org

Ken Cockburn recently edited the bilingual anthology of football haiku *The Season Sweetens / Die Saison Versüssend* for The Caseroom Press. He has contributed several translations to the forthcoming Carcanet/Scottish Poetry Library anthology *The night begins with a question: XXV Austrian Poems 1978–2002*.

Belinda Cooke's poetry, reviews and Russian translations have been published widely. She is currently completing an edition of *The Selected Poems of Marina Tsvetaeva*. She lives in Aberdeenshire.

Ellen Coverdale is a writer and translator of Irish descent. She lives and works mainly in rural France.

Andy Croft's books include *Red Letter Days, Out of the Old Earth, A Weapon in the Struggle, Selected Poems of Randall Swingler, Comrade Heart* and thirty-two books for teenagers, mostly about football. He has edited the anthologies *Red Sky at Night* (with Adrian Mitchell), *North by North East* (with Cynthia Fuller) and *Not Just a Game* (with Sue Dymoke) and published six books of poetry – *Nowhere Special, Gaps Between Hills, Headland, Just as Blue, Great North* and *Comrade Laughter*. He runs Smokestack Books and lives in Middlesbrough.

Anna Crowe was born in Plymouth in 1945 and brought up in France and Sussex. She studied at the University of St Andrews and has lived in the town since 1986. She co-founded *StAnza,* Scotland's Poetry Festival, and was its Artistic Director for its first seven years. She is the translator of Joan Margarit's *Tugs in the Fog.* Twice winner of the Peterloo competition, she has published three collections of her own poems, most recently *Punk with Dulcimer* (Peterloo 2006).

Damian Walford Davies lectures in the English Department at the University of Wales, Aberystwyth. His poems have appeared in *Poetry Wales, Oxford Poetry, English, The Oxford Magazine,* the Clutag Press leaflet series, and *Planet.* A co-authored collection, *Whiteout* (with Richard Marggraf Turley) will be published by Parthian in 2007. He is completing a second collection, *Suit of Lights.*

Ulrike Draesner was born in Munich in 1962. She studied English, Philosophy and German literature in Munich and Oxford Her first book, a collection of poetry, appeared in 1995. Since then she has published three volumes of poetry, including *kugel blitz* (ball lightning) (2005), three novels, mostly recently *Spiele* (Games) (2005), and two volumes of short stories. Draesner also works as a translator (Gertrude Stein, Hilda Doolittle, Louise Glück) and writes essays on media and cultural change. Since 1996 she has lived in Berlin. See www.draesner.de.

Andrew Duncan was born in Leeds, in 1956. Books of poetry include: *Pauper Estate* and *The Imaginary in Geometry*. He has translated poems by Thomas Kling, Lutz Seiler, and Erich Arendt, amongst others. Co-editor and chief poetry translator for *New Writing in German* (special issue of *Chicago Review*, 2002).

Peter France is Professor Emeritus of French at the University of Edinburgh. He has published widely on French and Russian literature and is editor of the *Oxford Guide to Literature in English Translation* and the *Oxford History of Literary Translation in English*. Many of his translations of Aygi are published in the three volumes, *Selected Poems*, 1954–1994 (Angel Books, 1997), *Salute – to Singing* (Zephyr Books, 2002), and *Child-and-Rose* (New Directions, 2003). A further volume, *Field-Russia*, will be published by New Directions in 2007.

Iain Galbraith's recent poems have appeared in the *T L S*, *New Writing 14*, *PN Review*, *Best Scottish Poems 2005* and *The Allotment. New Lyric Poets* (Stride, 2006). He is a widely published translator of German poetry, and has edited and co-translated two dual-language anthologies: *The Night Begins with a Question. Austrian Poetry* (Carcanet, 2007), and *Intime Weiten. XXV Schottische Gedichte* (Folio, Vienna, 2006).

Lavinia Greenlaw has published three books of poems, most recently *Minsk*, and two novels: *Mary George of Allnorthover* and *An Irresponsible Age*. Her work for BBC radio includes programmes about the Arctic and the Baltic, the solstices and equinoxes, and several dramas. She has also written three libretti and two song cycles, and her first book of non-fiction,

The Importance of Music to Girls, will appear in 2007. She teaches at Goldsmiths College, University of London.

Peter Hainsworth taught Italian at Oxford until he retired in 2003. He has written on a wide range of Italian authors. Most recently he co-edited with David Robey the *Oxford Companion to Italian Literature* (2002). He has all but completed a translation of a selection of Petrarch's poems and prose.

David Hart, lives in Birmingham UK, born Aberystwyth, sometime university chaplain, theatre critic, arts administrator, now freelance poet, with part-time posts at Warwick and Birmingham universities, residencies include psychiatric and general hospitals and Worcester Cathedral; Birmingham Poet Laureate 1997-98. Books of poetry include *Setting the poem to words; Crag Inspector; Work, the work,* and, forthcoming from Five Seasons Press, *Running out.*

Michael Hofmann was born in 1957 in Freiburg, Germany and came to England in 1957. Since reading English and researching at Cambridge University, from 1983 he has worked as a freelance writer: editing, reviewing, translating over forty works from the German including *Ashes for Breakfast* by Durs Grünbein, and publishing four prize-winning collections of poems, most recently *Approximately Nowhere* (Faber 1999). He teaches each spring semester at the University of Florida.

Lakshmi Holmström is a writer and translator of contemporary Tamil literature. Her publications include a re-telling of the fifth-century Tamil narrative poems *Silappadikaram and Manimekalai,* and *The inner courtyard,* a collection of short stories by Indian women. Royal Literary Fund writing fellow, University of East Anglia, 2003–6. Currently working on a book of Tamil poetry in translation.

Robert Hull's work has been published in *The Interpreter's House, Smiths Knoll, The Cumberland Poetry Review*, and elsewhere. His *Encouraging Shakespeare* was published by Peterloo Poets; a second volume is due out from Peterloo in spring 2007. He has also written many books for children, including two single-author verse collections, *Stargrazer* from Hodder, and *Everest and Chips* from OUP. His *Behind the Poem* is an acclaimed full-length study of the process of children writing poems in classrooms.

Naomi Jaffa was born in London 1961 and lives in Suffolk. Her first pamphlet collection *The Last Hour of Sleep* was published by Five Leaves Press in 2003. She has worked for The Poetry Trust – the organisation which runs the Aldeburgh Poetry Festival plus a year round programme of readings, education projects, residential courses and publishing initiatives – since 1993. She succeeded its founder, Michael Laskey, as director in 1999.

Francis R. Jones has published twelve books of translated poetry from Dutch, Bosnian-Croatian-Serbian, Hungarian and Russian. He has won several UK and international poetry translation prizes, the latest being the 2005 James Brockway Prize for his versions of the Dutch poet Hans Faverey. As a day job, he lectures and researches in translation studies at Newcastle University.

Desirée Jung was born and raised in Brazil and now is also a citizen of Canada. She began her career as a journalist but fell in love with translation when she moved to Vancouver, BC, and began translating the Canadian poet P. K. Page into Brazilian Portuguese. She is currently working on the translation from the Portuguese into English of selected works by the Angolan writer Gonçalo M. Tavares.

Mimi Khalvati was born in Iran and grew up on the Isle of Wight. Her five Carcanet collections include her *Selected Poems* (2000) and *The Chine* (2002). She is the founder of The Poetry School and has co-edited its anthologies of new writing published by Enitharmon Press. She currently holds a Royal Literary Fund fellowship at City University. In 2006 she received a Cholmondeley Award and a new collection, *The Meanest Flower*, is forthcoming in 2007.

Tom Kuhn is general editor of the English Brecht edition in the 'Methuen Drama' series, now published by A&C Black. He has edited and translated several volumes in the series, including (with Steve Giles) *Brecht on Art and Politics* (2003). He is a Fellow of St Hugh's College, Oxford.

Karen Leeder is Reader in German at the University of Oxford, and Fellow and Tutor in German at New College, Oxford and has published widely on modern German literature, especially poetry, including (with Tom Kuhn) *Empedocles' Shoe: Essays on Brecht's Poetry*. She has also translated work by a number of German writers, including an anthology of poems, *After Brecht: A Celebration*, for Carcanet Press in 2006. Her translations of Evelyn Schlag's *Selected Poems* (Carcanet, 2004) won the Schlegel-Tieck Prize 2005.

Elizabeth MacDonald teaches English and Translation at Pisa University. Her collection of short stories, *A House of Cards*, is due for publication with Pillar Press in September 2006.

Adrian Mitchell is a poet, playwright, performer and writer of stories for both children and adults. He was born in London in 1932 and lives near Hampstead Heath with his wife Celia Hewitt, the actress, and his golden retriever, Daisy the Dog of Peace.

Dasha C. Nisula teaches Russian language and literature at Western Michigan University. She translates poetry from Russian and Croatian and thus far has published two books of poetry in translation. Her translations have appeared in *Pennsylvania Review*, *Colorado Review*, and *International Poetry Review* and elsewhere. She lives and works in Kalamazoo, Michigan.

Jeff Nosbaum's most recent publications include poems in *Poetry Review*, *Acumen* and *MPT* 3/5, and reviews in *Poetry Wales*. Originally from the US , he has spent the last dozen years in Britain and currently lives in Cheltenham.

Albert Ostermaier was born in Munich in 1967. He has published five collections of poetry, most recently, *Polar* (2006). Alongside poetry he is also the author of prose works and libretti and often works with the composer Bret Wrede. He is also a noted dramatist and was the dramatist in residence at the Bavarian State Theatre during the 1999–2000 season. In July 2006 he was artistic director of the five-day long poetry festival *abc Brecht: Brecht Augsburg Connected* in Augsburg, the city of Brecht's birth.

Bert Papenfuss was born in 1956 in Reuterstadt Stavenhagen, GDR. After working as an electrician and lighting technician he became a freelance writer in 1980. One of the leading writers of the avant-garde underground culture in the former East Germany, he has published over 20 collections of poetry, most recently (2005) *Rumbalotte. Gedichte 1998–2002*. Since 1999 he has been co-director of the bar and club, Kaffee Burger, a popular alternative music and literature venue in Berlin.

Pascale Petit's last two collections, *The Huntress* (Seren, 2005) and *The Zoo Father* (Seren, 2001, Poetry Book Society Recommendation), were both shortlisted for the TS Eliot Prize and were Books of the Year in the *Times Literary Supplement*. A prize-winning pamphlet *The Wounded Deer – Fourteen poems after Frida Kahlo* (Smith Doorstop) was also published in 2005. In 2004 she was selected as a Next Generation Poet.

Anna Reckin's poetry and essays have been published in the US and the UK. She has just finished collaborating on an English translation of Cristina Peri Rossi's *Strategies of Desire*.

Oliver Reynolds is an usher at the Royal Opera House. His last book of poems was *Almost* (1999).

Lucy Wilkinson studied Illustration at Manchester School of Art, and English Literature at Oxford University, and holds a Postgraduate Diploma in Theatre Design from Bristol Old Vic Theatre School. She works freelance as an Illustrator and Theatre Designer, and her work has been short-listed for both the Macmillan Children's Book Prize and the Linbury Prize for Theatre Design. She illustrates poetry for adults and children, and fiction for all ages, including publications by OUP, Usborne Books, Signal Books, Holywell Press and Delos Press. She contributes the cover designs for each new issue of *MPT*.

Derk Wynand, Professor Emeritus at the University of Victoria, BC, and former editor of *The Malahat Review*, has published ten collections of poetry, one of fiction, and five translated from the German of HC Artmann, Erich Wolfgang Skwara and Dorothea Grünzweig. His translations of Dorothea Grünzweig's versions of Four Mansi Songs appeared in *MPT* 3/5; other poems by her, in his translation, are to be found in *The Malahat Review, CV2* and *Prism International*.

MODERN POETRY IN TRANSLATION   Series 3   Number 1

INTRODUCTIONS

Edited by David and Helen Constantine
Cover by Chris Hyde

Contents

Price £11
Available from www.mptmagazine.com

MODERN POETRY IN TRANSLATION   Series 3   Number 2

DIASPORA

Edited by David and Helen Constantine
Cover by Lucy Wilkinson

Contents
Editorial   David and Helen Constantine

Reviews

Price £11
Available from www.mptmagazine.com

MODERN POETRY IN TRANSLATION   Series 3   Number 3

METAMORPHOSES

Edited by David and Helen Constantine
Cover by Lucy Wilkinson

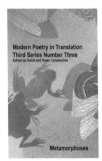

Contents
Editorial   David and Helen Constantine

Reviews

Antony Wood on Angela Livingstone's *Poems from Chevengur*

Josephine Balmer on Cliff Ashcroft's *Dreaming of Still Water* and Peter Boyle's *Eugenio Montejo*

Paschalis Nikolaou on Philip Ramp's *Karouzos*

Francis Jones on Jan Twardowski (translated by Sarah Lawson and Malgorzata Koraszweska) and *A Fine Line: New Poetry from Central and Eastern Europe*

Price £11
Available from www.mptmagazine.com

MODERN POETRY IN TRANSLATION   Series 3   Number 4

BETWEEN THE LANGUAGES

Edited by David and Helen Constantine

Cover by Lucy Wilkinson

Contents

Reviews
Olivier Burckhardt on Claire Malroux's *Birds and Bison*, translated by Marilyn Hacker
Sasha Dugdale on Ileana Mălăncioiu's, *After the Raising of Lazarus,* translated by Eiléan Ní Chuilleanáin

Price £11
Available from www.mptmagazine.com

MODERN POETRY IN TRANSLATION   Series 3   Number 5

TRANSGRESSIONS

Edited by David and Helen Constantine

Cover by Lucy Wilkinson

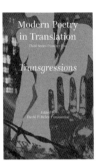

Contents
Editorial   David and Helen Constantine

Günter Grass, 'The Ballerina', translated by Michael Hamburger

Robert Hull, One Good Translation Deserves Another

Reviews
Olivia McCannon on Peter Dale's Tristan Corbière
Timothy Adès on Colin Sydenham's Horace
Paschalis Nikolaou on Richard Burns
Belinda Cooke on *Sailor's Home: A Miscellany of Poetry*, and Piotr Sommer's *Continued.*

Shorter Reviews and Further Books Received

Price £11
Available from www.mptmagazine.com

MPT Subscription Form

Name	Address
Phone	Postcode
E-mail	Country

I would like to subscribe to *Modern Poetry in Translation* (please tick relevant box):

Subscription Rates (including postage by surface mail)

	UK	Overseas
❏ One year subscription (2 issues)	£22	£26 / US$ 48
❏ Two year subscription (4 issues) with discount	£40	£48 / US$ 88

Student Discount*

	UK	Overseas
❏ One year subscription (2 issues)	£16	£20 / US$ 37
❏ Two year subscription (4 issues)	£28	£36 / US$ 66

Please indicate which year you expect to complete your studies 20 . . .

Standing Order Discount (only available to UK subscribers)

❏ Annual subscription (2 issues)	£20
❏ Student rate for annual subscription (2 issues)*	£14

Payment Method (please tick appropriate box)

❏ **Cheque:** please make cheques payable to: *Modern Poetry in Translation.*
Sterling, US Dollar and Euro cheques accepted.

❏ **Standing Order:** please complete the standing order request below, indicating
the date you would like your first payment to be taken. This should be at least one
month after you return this form. We will set this up directly with your bank.
Subsequent annual payments will be taken on the same date each year. For UK only.

Bank Name	Account Name
Branch Address	❏ Please notify my bank
	Please take my first payment on
Post Code	......./......./......... and future payments on
Sort Code	the same date each year.
Account Number	Signature:
	Date........./......./...........

Bank Use Only: In favour of Modern Poetry in Translation, Lloyds TSB,
1 High St, Carfax, Oxford, OX1 4AA, UK a/c 03115155 Sort-code 30-96-35

Please return this form to: The Administrator, Modern Poetry in Translation, The Queen's
College, Oxford, OX1 4AW   administrator@mptmagazine/www.mptmagazine.com